'Daniel Browne's book is a must-read for anyone who has ever felt tired of being tired. Through compelling examples, and practical exercises, The Energy Equation is the kick-start to living your life with passion!' Steven D'Souza, author of Brilliant Networking, **www.brilliantnetworking.net**

The Energy Equation

How to be a top performer without burning yourself out

Daniel Browne

PEARSON

Harlow, England • London • New York • Boston • San Francisco • Toronto • Sydney
Auckland • Singapore • Hong Kong • Tokyo • Seoul • Taipei • New Delhi
Cape Town • São Paulo • Mexico City • Madrid • Amsterdam • Munich • Paris • Milan

PEARSON EDUCATION LIMITED

Edinburgh Gate
Harlow CM20 2JE
Tel: +44 (0)1279 623623
Website: www.pearson.com/uk

First published in 2013 (print and electronic)

© Pearson Education Limited 2013 (print and electronic)

The right of Daniel Browne to be identified as author of this work has been asserted by him in accordance with the Copyright, Designs and Patents Act 1988.

Pearson Education is not responsible for the content of third-party internet sites.

ISBN: 978-0-273-77601-7 (print)
      978-0-273-78147-9 (PDF)
      978-0-273-78146-2 (ePub)

British Library Cataloguing-in-Publication Data
A catalogue record for this book is available from the British Library

Library of Congress Cataloging-in-Publication Data
Browne, Daniel, 1975-
  The energy equation : how to be a top performer without burning yourself out / Daniel Browne.
      pages cm
  Includes index.
  ISBN 978-0-273-77601-7 (pbk.)
  1. Job stress. 2. Burn out (Psychology) 3. Performance. 4. Time management. 5. Vitality. I. Title.
  HF5548.85.B763 2013
  650.1--dc23

The screenshots in this book are reprinted by permission of Microsoft Corporation.

10 9 8 7 6 5 4 3 2 1
16 15 14 13 12

Illustrations on pp. 16 and 71 by Adrian Cartwright (Planet illustration) and all other cartoons by Bill Piggins.

Cover design by Dan Mogford.

Print edition typeset in 11pt Helevetica Neue Light by 30.
Print edition printed and bound in Great Britain by Henry Ling Ltd., at Dorset Press, Dorchester, Dorset.

NOTE THAT ANY PAGE CROSS REFERENCES REFER TO THE PRINT EDITION

Contents

About the author

A consultant in business strategy and personal productivity, Daniel has worked with both blue chip organisations and entrepreneurial firms.

The idea for this book came from his early career as an investment banker, and later as a strategy consultant. Here he experienced the culture of extremely long hours typical of city workers, working 70–100 hours most weeks.

He started trying to find a way to sleep less and work more. This quickly became a quest to see if it was possible to increase productivity, energy and wellbeing while working in a long-hours environment. The lessons he learnt on this quest form the foundations of this book.

Daniel's blog can be found at **www.danielebrowne.com** and twitter is danielebrowne.

Acknowledgements

This book has been helped by the support, contribution and encouragement of others. So first to those who provided valuable input and feedback I'd like to thank Michelle Watts, Panita Vig, Anne Lamerton, Pavel Mikolowski, Steven D'Souza and Melanie Flory.

To my rocks for all the support and encouragement, a big thanks and lots of love to my mother, father and sister, Riaz Hussein, Sufiya Patel, Nigel Camp, Desmond Moeira, Daniel Priestley, Emma Ponsonby and Jacquie Moses.

Preface

This text is the product of 10 years of research, personal experience and the teachings of various mentors. In that time, I experienced some of the longest working hours, like many people who work in the city (usually investment bankers, management consultants and city lawyers). It started immediately after leaving university. With good grades from a good university, I launched my career straight into the corporate finance department of an investment bank. In my first month I experienced a major shock to the system: my typical hours were from 9am to 9pm daily, which regularly extended past 11pm. Working all night until morning, going home to shower, and returning to work was not an uncommon occurrence.

Fancying something a bit more sedate, with regular hours, my second job was better – a nine to five. However, in reality, to do the job well meant working beyond these hours. Soon the late hour creep came in. In busy times the hours would extend past 6pm to 8 or even 9pm. The problem was that the 'busy times' became more frequent until 'busy' was the norm. This is how most management jobs are nowadays.

Thinking job number three would be better, I worked for a consultancy with a boss who would go through creative phases of working from 7am until 11pm. Being the junior, I had to stay up and assist him. I often believed that my life was destined to consist of six-day weeks, long hours and a limited social life. During the worst of times, I wished I could just step into an alternate dimension where time stood still, enjoy a full eight hours of sleep at night, and come back to reality with barely any time passing.

As this was not possible, I began to explore ways to increase my productivity so I could stay effective during those long working hours and get more done so that I could enjoy a social life. I have always believed in having my cake and eating it too, and I could never stand being trapped or limited. I believe it is possible to have a great job *and* a great life. By learning meditation, breathing exercises and certain energy techniques, I learned how to keep my body operating efficiently and my energy levels high and sustained. I learned from one of the masters of productivity how to be more productive in life and how to maintain my focus and concentration. Out of all of this work, I noticed the similarities between many of the traditions of yoga, tai chi and meditation, and I began to extract the things that worked and resonated with me. Currently, neuroscience experts and consciousness studies are revealing the secrets that many yogi and tai chi masters have known all along: that the brain is a powerful thing and can be trained and harnessed to increase your IQ, your power of focus, and even accelerate recovery and healing of the body. While studying brain science, things really started to open up for me. I began pushing my body through the boundaries of what I knew about wellbeing, energy and performance. I discovered how to sleep better, work more productively, have more energy, and even how to get rid of certain ailments. I learnt how to get 'into the zone' more consistently and how to be more productive and get results.

At first, I didn't see the value in sharing all of this training. It was purely my personal quest to unlock my own potential and to achieve an edge in my work. However, after speaking to many overworked, stressed bankers, lawyers and teachers, I started to see the value in sharing my experiences and research. I began teaching people about peak performance, but soon realised that many people don't have the time to practise yoga and meditation or to attend a seminar. This is why I decided to write this text.

I still work long hours from time to time (although now I work for myself), and it doesn't seem like 'work' at all. However, using what I have learned, I get a lot more done than I used to, and I am filled with the kind of fulfilment and satisfaction one gets from doing one's best.

This text is designed to give you some shortcuts to getting 'into the zone'. If you allow it, it can lead you on your journey to more effectiveness, peace of mind, and freedom. Your progress will be variable, as some things will be easy for you and some will take more time for you to understand. It depends on where you start – there are always higher levels to reach.

While the main premise of this text is work productivity, ultimately it is about having a life that works for you. Because we spend most of our time at work, it is the main factor that determines our quality of life. Therefore, becoming more productive at work can have a huge impact on the quality of our lives.

Introduction

Do you feel as if you're heading towards a world of 'over-whelm': that there is way too much information to absorb; too much to do and not enough time in which to do it?

There are many factors that have contributed, but we have gradually drifted into a culture of immediacy. The recent recession, company efficiency drives and cost savings have increased the workload for everyone, while the time in which to do it has decreased. The speed of work has also increased. Companies have become more competitive. Responsiveness and the ability to prove that you can get back to your client faster than your competitors has added to the workload; add that to the need to deliver excellence and we have a picture of too much work, not enough resources and not enough time to meet the new demands.

In the late 1990s and early 2000s you would make a request of someone by email and expect a response in a few days, but the advent of mobile email, 'Blackberries' and instant messaging means the expectation of a timely response has increased. We are expected to respond sooner and we expect people to get back to us sooner.

How many unread messages are in your inbox? For many, email inboxes have become unmanageable. In addition to our email, we now have a new information source in the form of social media, which make it possible to spend even more time online.

The current working culture presents two main problems:

1 We do not have enough time and when we have any 'free' time we are too exhausted to fully enjoy it, spending it recovering rather than living.

2 We are often stressed and overwhelmed. With tight deadlines and an overload of information, stress is unavoidable. Stress has now become the most common cause of long-term sickness absence according to the Chartered Institute of Personnel and Development (CIPD).

So, imagine a different world. In this world we would work more effectively, not to death. This is a world where we would bring our best to work, where we would use our whole brain, and where we would be fit and healthy. In this world we would be passionate about the work we do and would use our strengths and deal with our weaknesses, without being daunted by or ashamed of them. In this ideal world we would work in harmony with the design of our bodies. This world *does* exist and we may have had glimpses of it in the past. However we may have been so trapped in the world of overwork that we have forgotten it.

This text is a bridge to this world. There is a whole body of knowledge freely available of which most of us are unaware and not accessing.

We are in an age where there is so much more knowledge available. There are advances in elite sports science which teach us how the human body operates at optimal performance. We can use this to know how we can sleep better, regenerate more effectively and be fitter and healthier.

Advances in neuroscience show us how we can improve our brains: how we can become smarter, learning more rapidly and absorbing more information. In this way we can change our thinking, sleep better and eliminate stress.

Eastern practices such as yoga, tai chi and meditation which are now widely adopted in the West are scientifically proven to have a huge impact on our physical and mental wellbeing.

There is such a wealth of wisdom available, and this text brings some of that practical wisdom to the world of work. This will make work and life better *and* enable us to be more productive, have more playtime and fun, while gaining experience using our intellectual genius to live a fuller life.

The first step is being *willing* to step away from the world of overwork and the thinking that gets us trapped there. Our obsession with work has led to a loss of control. We think that by putting in more hours and being available all the time to respond to calls and emails we will get ahead. However, it only leads to greater dissatisfaction, stress and burnout. Unconsciously, we are trying to survive by meeting all the demands but when we stop and reflect, we know that it won't get any better. We require a new way of thinking. Are you ready to suspend the ways of the old world, to suspend all you know and change your thinking about work?

This text enables you to shift from the world of overwork to a more sustainable way of living and working.

As I said in the preface, this text is based on my experience 'in the trenches': the same trenches that many of you are in right now. I am referring to long work hours, with virtually no breaks, cranking out work like a machine most of the day. At night you try to get work out of your mind and get what little sleep you can. Such working hours are sadly becoming more normal in our culture.

This text will guide you into having more energy and vitality, increasing your level of performance and allowing you more available time for yourself. It is about putting more fuel in your tank.

Whether you want to have more energy in life, less stress and more time for yourself, or if you already lead an active lifestyle and are always on the go, this text is for you. In fact it was written with several kinds of people in mind.

The Os – The *O*verworked and *O*verwhelmed – those who want to get a better handle on what's on their plate. They want to have less stress, and more time for themselves and their families. This text will enable them to have more energy and vitality with less stress and help them to carve out more time for themselves.

The As – These are the *A*mbitious, *A*chieving, *A*lpha tribe, those who work a lot, yet want to be able to perform better still and get more done. This text will teach them how to push the boundaries of performance without sacrificing wellbeing. It is about sustainable competitiveness:

getting more effective sleep and reducing stress. They will learn how to get more done, while accessing the power of the brain.

The Bs – Busy **B**ees who rush around doing lots of things. Everyone knows this is a busy person, but they feel as though they're never quite there. They never feel they've accomplished a lot and don't have an overall picture of what they have achieved. This text will help them to focus on more meaningful accomplishment

The Ls – Learning **L**eaders – those who want to better themselves, their teams and their organisations. This text will teach them/you how to manage your own personal energy and help others to manage their own energy, increasing vitality, personal performance and organisational performance.

The Ss – Self Actualisers – those who are curious and would like improve their life by accessing the innate genius already present in their body and mind. They learn how to gain access to this, while learning to harness their own energy and improve their health and wellbeing.

The Gs – Go Getters – those who are already leading a full and active life with many pursuits and activities outside of work. This will show them how to put more fuel in the tank so they can do even more without exhausting themselves.

The Reluctant – those who have a concern about their capacity to get things done. Whether it's a concern about time or being overburdened, this text will help them go beyond the constraints of what they think is possible and to accomplish what they are capable of without exhausting themselves.

So which one are you? Or can you recognise yourself as being a mix of all these types? Do you want to have more of a life? Do you want more time for yourself or to spend with your family? Are you looking for a way to be more effective and get more done with less stress? Do you want to push the envelope in terms of your performance and gain a competitive edge? Would you like to overcome overwhelm? Would you like to transform the performance and vitality of your company? Which three are your most dominant thinking–behaviour patterns? What are your most pressing needs right now? Identifying which one you are will help you establish your energy and productivity needs.

THE ENERGY SCALE

Imagine a line of your energy starting from being completely burnt out to completely in flow. Along the way you pass (a) overworked, (b) just about coping, (c) doing ok, (d) performing well and (e) firing on all cylinders to (f) in flow – flow being the state where you are highly productive and creative, handling everything there is to do yet still having time to create a future.

We've all been there before, perhaps haphazardly. Getting to *flow* will not be a straight line. You'll find the goal posts move. You will have more responsibilities and more demands made on you, leading you back down to overwhelm. This may mean more responsibility at work or in your personal life (for example, starting a family or gaining a new addition to your family). Your life will expand. The demands will increase, so you'll need to have the energy to be able to meet them.

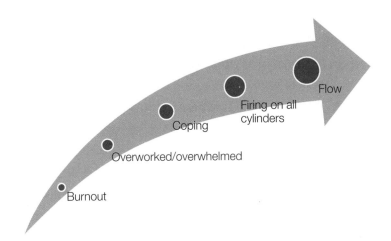

Flow

Firing on all
cylinders

Coping

Overworked/overwhelmed

Burnout

In fact your whole life has been and will continue to be about managing your energy.

This text will guide you on a journey to a new life as all of the concepts will effect a permanent change once you master them. Once you learn to manage your energy it is a life-long skill; you know when you are managing effectively and when you are not.

Once you learn how your body deals with stress you then have access to a world without stress and stress-related illness such as migraines, eye aches and muscle tensions. This is a world without the common mental and emotional issues we face, such as insomnia, chronic worry, anxiety and fear. This text will show you how to make a permanent shift.

HOW TO USE THIS TEXT

Given that you probably have a busy schedule, this text is designed to give you some shortcuts. We start with energy, as this is where the quickest win lies. Mastering the concepts simply requires the formation of new habits, as most exercises can be done in 5–20 minutes. Moreover, the practices in this book are very easy to fit into your schedule. You can do many of them while commuting or whenever you have idle time.

Your progress will be variable, as some things will be easy for you and some will take more time for you to understand. It depends on where you start as there are always higher levels to reach.

This text is in two sections. The first is about gaining quick wins: increasing energy, getting rid of stress, sleeping better and using your thinking at work. It is about dealing with the immediacy of overwork.

The second is a deeper look at how our view of the world impacts on what we do, how effective we are and what we really need to put into place to be more effective: how we can use that to transform our organisations.

The key concepts here are using the full power of our mind and body to help us have more in life.

CHAPTER 1

The energy cycle

I magine a continuum of energy. At the lowest level of energy we are in *'burnout'*, barely functioning. The highest level is *'flow'* the state where we are most productive. We may be very busy but we experience having the capacity to deal with everything and things seem to show up at the right time. Where would you be on this line?

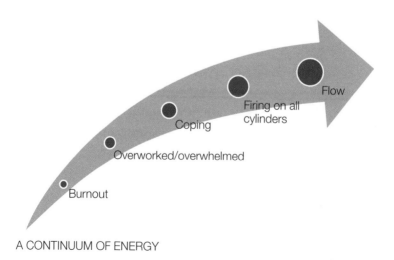

Flow

Firing on all
cylinders

Coping

Overworked/overwhelmed

Burnout

A CONTINUUM OF ENERGY

Most people are in the region of overworked to coping, which looks like this: the average working person after a day's work is often too exhausted to do anything other than eat, watch a bit of TV, maybe surf the internet a little and go to bed.

If they are motivated, they may go to the gym or meet up with a friend a few nights a week. However, they spend most of their evenings recovering from a long and often stressful day at work as well as spending the weekend recuperating from a stressful work week. Relaxation and rejuvenation should not be confused with recuperation. Many people would like to do more than 'veg out' but have no physical or mental energy to do much else than recuperate.

Firing on all cylinders to flow would be having around 15 hours of energy and vitality during the day. That would mean feeling energised from the time you get up to just short of the time you go to bed, let's say between 7am and about 9pm. Now if you're spending 8–10 of those hours at work then you get the remaining five hours to do whatever you want. Imagine finishing work at a reasonable time and feeling energised and excited. Would you just go home to eat, watch TV and go to bed? If you had three more hours of fuel in the tank wouldn't you make the most of it? You could have fun, study, learn a new language, work out, take a class, go ice-skating or dancing, have a massage, or something else.

You'll discover how you can access this. But first let's look at the stress cycle.

STRESS CYCLE – MY STORY

During a particular busy time at work I noticed I had become trapped in a cycle of stress. As I got busier, I started to work harder and for longer hours. This increased my stress levels but decreased my performance, prompting me to work even more to maintain my output. With increasing stress and declining performance I started making silly mistakes and began to lose confidence in my own abilities, causing a further drop in performance. This came to a head when I realised I would soon be fired so I asked to be transferred to another department where I could start over with something new.

When we are in particularly stressful periods we often find ourselves trapped in a cycle of stress. When we are stressed we don't sleep that well. This can range from sleeping badly through the night, to full bouts of insomnia where we are awake most of the night. The result of not sleeping well is that we wake up tired. We have a poor start to the day and feel low on energy. As a result of this low energy we are less alert and less vital; our pace and productivity suffers. Faced with a demanding day we feel stressed and frantic. By the end of the working day we feel exhausted and leave work annoyed, frustrated and upset. Either we didn't complete what we wanted to complete or we had to work later than we wanted in order to complete it. The evening is pretty much wasted as we're low on energy and are worried consciously or unconsciously about work. This worry affects our sleep, which means we don't sleep well, repeating the cycle for the next day.

We usually endure this type of stress cycle for days or even weeks until the busy period eases up, or we take ourselves out of the situation, or worse we become ill or burnt out.

THE STRESS CYCLE

Many high performance workers are strong willed and able to survive this stress cycle for long periods of time without burnout, but with minor bouts of colds, flu and other symptoms. The typical response is to medicate ourselves through this and use force of will to keep going. However, over long periods of time, living like this can cause you to slip into the **chronic stress cycle**.

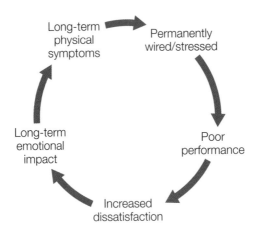

Long-term
physical
symptoms

Permanently
wired/stressed

Poor
performance

Increased
dissatisfaction

Long-term
emotional
impact

CHRONIC STRESS CYCLE

The human physiology is only supposed to handle stress for short periods of time. Over a long period of time, the body gets used to the chemicals (adrenaline and glucocortisoids) produced by stress and we become desensitised to stress. Stress becomes the norm and we form a dependency on the chemicals of stress. In effect we are dependent on our stress. This sort of chemical dependency is the same as other addictive behaviours such as gambling, drugs, etc. The chemicals produced, be they dopamine, adrenaline or others, become a requirement for the body. Any chemical dependence will lead to a downward spiral of decreasing performance, energy and physical and mental wellbeing leading to longer-term impacts on our health. Most people live in a slow low-level variant of this stress cycle – enough to survive on without too many long-term effects. However, there is the danger of longer-term illness.

Traditionally stress management has been about breaking the stress cycle, which is effective in its aim. However, whenever you are managing something negative the best you can get to is 100% effective management and that requires work. There is always the potential to backslide if management is not effective or maintained. It's like managing time. As soon as you stop managing time you get back to losing time. There is a law that says what you focus on increases, so when you focus on managing stress what you get is less stress when you are effective or more stress when you are not. Managing stress becomes a dominating concept and your life is consumed with it. When you focus on positive outcomes the problems you are dealing with tend to disappear. So when you focus on what you would like rather than focusing on getting less stressed you'll find stress becomes less of a concern. In other words, focusing on a positive replacement for stress will lessen your stress.

ENERGY CYCLE

So what should we focus on instead? Well, the opposite of stress is energy and vitality. Just as there is a cycle of stress there is a cycle of energy. If we take steps to reverse the effects of the stress cycle – if we focus on getting great sleep, if we eliminate the effects of poor sleep, if we increase concentration and focus, if we learn to let go of worry, if we learn to energise the body – what we get is a cycle of energy: a cycle of increasing energy, vitality, focus and productivity.

In this text we'll cover the practices that negate and reverse the effects of the stress cycle and which actually increase your performance, productivity and wellbeing. So how do we get to an energy cycle? Take any element of the stress cycle and create a practice to produce the opposite and you will get the following:

- A poor start to the day becomes an energised start to the day.
- Instead of poor productivity we actively take steps to increase focus and intention and we continually replenish our energy throughout the day.
- Instead of becoming worried we de-stress and clear out our mind.
- Instead of being unable to sleep or getting poor sleep we learn how to get effective sleep.

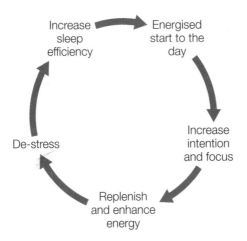

THE ENERGY CYCLE

Over the long term this becomes an ever-improving cycle, leading to greater physical, emotional and mental wellbeing only limited by the extent of practise that one brings to it. The opposite of the chronic stress cycle would look like the long-term energy cycle.

So the four key stages are learning to

1 increase energy;

2 improve sleep or maximise on our sleep efficiency;

3 focus the mind and concentrate;

4 de-stress or free the mind of worry.

We will go through each one of these stages in this text.

Peace of
mind and
enjoyment
in life

Physical
wellbeing

Increased
capacity for
energy and
vitality

Greater
achievement

Increased
productivity

LONG-TERM ENERGY CYCLE

CHAPTER 2

The energy equation – E is for energy

ENERGY

Energy is defined as one's capacity to work and take physical and mental action at work or play, and feelings of vitality and enthusiasm for life. Our level of energy is obviously important: the more energy and vitality we have the better we feel, the more we can do and the faster we can do it. The more productive we are at work, the more we can devote to life outside work.

At work, energy determines the speed and ease with which we get things done. Have you noticed the staff at Pret a Manger or McDonald's? The speed at which they serve customers is pretty amazing; they have a high level of energy and an efficiency that is unmatched in other fast-food restaurants. Contrast this with the average restaurant or coffee shop, where the staff are less focused in their energy and often unmotivated and not engaged.

Notice a master chef at work or an experienced barista making coffee, and you will see their focused motion. They channel their energy into what they are doing, and their work becomes a graceful dance.

Now think of the number of times you've had a full day ahead of you but had no energy for it or you felt annoyed, frustrated or drained at work? Did your day feel wasted?

Conversely, how many times have you been bursting with energy with a full day ahead of you and felt that you were ready for anything? How much more did you accomplish? How much more enjoyment do you have when you're in a state of high energy?

How much you accomplish varies, depending on your energy levels. Managing and focusing your energy is also important. If your energy is all over the place, or unfocused, you won't accomplish as much as someone who is focused.

Another important factor here is how energy affects the way we come across to others. People can sense when we're raring to go or when we're tired and fed up and that can make a real difference to how they relate to us. Charismatic people tend to have high levels of energy whether it's a frenetic energy or a calm gentle aura. It feels as though their energy projects outwards. If you are constantly overlooked at work or you don't stand out it may be a good idea to look at how much energy you have. How do you feel when you're around a tired or stressed person? You pick up on it and it affects you. The impact may vary from you altering your mood to match or lift theirs or just wanting to move away from that person. So outside of work, if you are coming home exhausted every day remember that you are having a negative impact on your partner.

THE ENERGY EQUATION

The human body is like a light bulb which converts electricity into light. In the same way our body converts the food we eat into physical energy and heat.

However, light bulbs are not totally efficient. Not all of the electricity goes into producing light; some also goes into producing heat, which is an unwanted effect. In the same way, not all of the energy we use is useful energy, some of it is unwanted. So where does this unwanted energy go? In our case it's not wasted as heat. Instead it gets lost as stress and tension.

For example, when you sit at a desk in an uncomfortable position, you are wasting energy using muscles in your shoulders and back. Your body tenses muscles which don't need to be used; the result is tension or even pain.

With a light bulb the efficiency loss is due to the resistance of the heating element; if you lower the resistance of the heating element you have more energy for light. For the human body, if we lower the resistance, which is mainly stress, we increase our efficiency. This leads us to the energy equation for the body:

> ### THE ENERGY EQUATION
>
> $$E = P - R$$
>
> P = Peak energy
>
> R = Resistance to the flow of energy

Energy = **P**eak energy minus **R**esistance

Peak physical energy – the energy we have available due to our physical body.

Resistance – the resistance to that energy flowing or being utilised. This is stress or tension.

So, the way to increase your energy is to increase your peak physical energy and reduce your stress.

INCREASING PHYSICAL ENERGY

Peak physical energy is influenced by a variety of factors, most of which you'll know and are common sense: primarily exercise, food and rest.

As humans we have a great potential for physical energy. Take ultra endurance runner, Stu Mittleman; he once ran 1,000 miles in 11 days and 19 hours. He would run for 21 hours a day and sleep only three hours in 24.

A little bit closer to home, hard-working seminar speakers like Tony Robbins spend 10 to 15 hours a day, 200 days a year speaking on stage in their seminars.

These extraordinary people demonstrate our potential peak physical energy when we work on training ourselves. So if it's superhuman levels of energy that you want, you could choose to train like an athlete. However, most of us don't need to go to such extremes; some simple exercises can make a difference. Here are the key elements:

Exercise: There is a plethora of advice about exercising – how much and what is good for us – but generally, if we exercise regularly we will have more energy. A good mixture of cardiovascular training, strength training and stretching (yoga or plain stretching) is recommended.

Adequate sleep: Giving your body adequate rest allows you to recover and rejuvenate yourself. Later in this text we will look at sleep in more detail and I'll show you how to push the envelope in terms of reducing the amount you sleep.

Food and nutrition: There is a huge wealth of advice available on food so I won't cover it in depth. I found what works for me by consulting a nutritionist and I can recommend this. The main thing is to avoid dips in energy by ensuring that you have balanced blood sugar levels.

Too often busy office workers will grab sugary snacks or refined carbohydrates for an energy pick-me-up. These foods release a lot of energy quickly as all the sugar rushes into your bloodstream. So you get a quick hit of energy. Then your pancreas kicks in, producing insulin to return your blood sugar levels to normal. You then feel sleepy as your brain releases serotonin, hence the energy slump afterwards. So these quick fixes actually make you less energetic. Also frequent blood sugar spikes tax your pancreatic organs, putting you more at risk of diabetes.

What you actually need is slow release carbohydrates such as brown rice, oats, quinoa and other whole foods that release energy into the system in a consistent and manageable way. Eating protein, fat and vegetables with carbohydrates prevents high energy spikes. Avoid white carbohydrates like sugar, bread, white rice and potatoes.

Emotions: When we are excited and passionate about something we find we have more energy. Our bodies release endorphins which make us feel good and more energised. When we are feeling depressed we tend to have low energy. (In later chapters we will explore this a bit more.)

REDUCING RESISTANCE

It makes sense to do as much as possible to increase the peak energy side of the energy equation. You can get gains with correct nutrition, exercise and emotions. But it is just as important to reduce the stress side of the equation. Reducing stress will have a profound impact on your life: you'll sleep better, be more level-headed and have improved wellbeing.

Most of us will have a certain level of resistance to the flow of energy in our bodies. These are learned tensions which we may carry for a short time. For example, if you have permanently tight muscles in your back or shoulders you are carrying that tension even if you're not stressed.

People generally don't notice their constant state of tension until they totally relax or get feedback from a masseur or physiotherapist. So even if you think you don't have any stress consider that there is stress somewhere; you just haven't got to that level of sensitivity to be able to detect it.

So there is the physical stress and resistance that we are familiar with but also emotional resistance. Emotional resistance refers to all the unpleasant emotions we have that, over time, make us feel stressed or worn out. In a work environment this includes anxiety, conflict, frustration, or even boredom. Whenever you are in a prolonged negative emotional state your energy gets used up in keeping this state. There are physical sensations attached to negative emotions. Just notice how your body feels when you are angry. You'll feel a knot in your stomach or tension in your head – all diversions of peak energy.

Another form of emotional resistance occurs when you use your energy to be something you are not, suppress your emotions, or hide who you truly are. A common but hopefully changing example is women who suppress their femininity to fit into a macho work environment. Over time, putting in the effort to be something that is not in line with what you really feel requires effort and can deplete your energy. Ask any trained actor; acting requires energy. So if you feel there is an uncomfortable environment at work it's an idea to look at where your energy is going.

In the Western world the mental/emotional side of our energy is not taken into consideration or very well understood. The mind is the biggest tool we have to harness energy; our minds have a greater control over the body than we realise. As you will learn later on in this text, we can literally make ourselves feel more tired or more energised with just a thought and we'll uncover how the limitations we put upon ourselves impact on our energy. For example, the biggest limitation to our capacity for energy is psychological, not physical.

MASTERING BREATHING

Before all of this though we need to go right back to basics, in fact to one of the most basic things we learn as a newborn baby: mastering breathing.

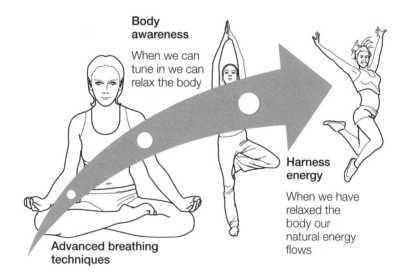

Body awareness
When we can tune in we can relax the body

Advanced breathing techniques

Harness energy
When we have relaxed the body our natural energy flows

Of course we all know how to breathe. However, not everyone does it correctly. It is amazing how many people have problems that arise because they are shallow breathers. I have met people who, after learning to breathe properly, have cured themselves of anxiety, headaches and stress-related illnesses.

Breathing for energy requires a different way of breathing. We need to make a conscious effort at first, but after a while breathing for energy starts to feel natural. To do it correctly, you must allow your lungs to fill up with air. How many times do people say, 'Take a deep breath' to someone who is under a lot of stress? Your body needs to breathe deeply in order to feel energised and relaxed. Learned deep-breathing techniques are essential parts of yoga and tai chi. Deep breathing is a great antidote to stress, as it helps you relax and increase your energy. Practise the following breathing exercises; they may seem simple but are critical.

Note: all the exercises in this chapter should be done sequentially. It is recommended you master each exercise before moving on to the next one. The sequence helps you tune in to your body and become more sensitive to your underlying level of stress.

Breathing Exercise 1: Breathing 101

This is an exercise to test and correct your breathing.

1 Stand up straight, lie down on your back, or sit with your back straight. Make sure you are comfortable and able to relax.

▶

2 Rest one hand on your chest and one hand on your stomach just below your ribs. Breathe as you always do and notice whether your chest rises and falls or if your stomach rises and falls.

3 If your stomach rises while your chest remains still, you are breathing correctly.

4 If your chest rises more than your stomach, correct your breathing by keeping your chest still and letting your breath fill your stomach first. Practise breathing in and out while you keep your hand on your stomach and ensure that your chest stays still. Take a deep breath and count to five before exhaling.

5 Keep doing these exercises so that you can learn to breathe this way all the time. This type of breathing will eventually become natural to you and won't require mental effort.

6 Use every opportunity to practise breathing – for example, while waiting in line somewhere, when you are on hold on the phone, or while you are at work, at your desk, or stuck in a traffic jam.

Breathing Exercise 2: Belly breathing

This exercise continues belly breathing but also enables you to expand your lung capacity and get a feeling of the power of your breath.

1 Start as above, in a comfortable position.

2 Inhale through your nose at an even rate and allow your stomach to push out. Again, if you wish, you can place your hand on your stomach.

3 Exhale slowly through your mouth and allow your stomach to return to its normal position. Exhaling should take the same time as inhaling.

4 Repeat.

5 To get even more breath, once your abdomen is full start to allow your lungs to fill, filling all the way to the top of your lungs into your shoulders. This is great for getting rid of tension in your shoulders. Breathing from the back of your lungs, into your rib cage, is a good way to expand your lung capacity, and it will help you relax even more.

6 If you feel any dizziness when breathing, return to normal breathing until you feel comfortable and then try again, but inhale and exhale less than before.

Now you may have noticed in these breathing exercises that you felt the air expand beyond where your physical lungs exist and it felt as if you were breathing into your belly. This is a common technique in a variety of disciplines including singing, yoga and tai chi. What is actually happening is that the diaphragm, located under the rib cage, expands downwards and your stomach pushes out. There is no breath going into your stomach but imagining that there is provides a good mental aid to help you to breathe correctly. If you had this sensation then that is perfect as it is one of the key ingredients to energising the body.

Whether you believe in Chi or not doesn't matter. Use it as a mental construct: imagine it. Imagination is a very powerful tool. With some mastery you'll be able to have the sensation of breathing into any part of the body and that body part relaxing and feeling more energised. So stay tuned for this.

BODY CONSCIOUSNESS

Correct breathing is the core foundation for energy – when you correct your breathing, everything else follows naturally. The next step on the road to increasing your energy is body consciousness. Here is a quick story to illustrate the point:

CASE STUDY

One summer, while working on an internship in Wales, I discovered how to eliminate headaches. I was working in an aluminium plant and living in a beautiful farmhouse in the middle of nowhere. There wasn't a lot to do outside of work, so at weekends I used to sit in the fields in contemplation and reflect on life. I was meditating before I even knew what meditation was. I discovered by accident a feeling of having muscles under my skull, on top of my brain. I noticed I could contract and relax these muscles, and that these muscles were the cause of my tension headaches. By relaxing the muscles, I could eliminate tension headaches. Since that time, I have hardly ever had a headache – the only exceptions have been from flu or eye problems (and those are rare occurrences, too). This was a result of becoming more conscious and sensitive to the muscles in the body. After that, I started developing a higher sensitivity in other areas of my body, particularly my eyes and my stomach. I could relieve eye strain by catching it a lot earlier; my eyesight even improved as a result. I was a lot more sensitive to tension in my stomach either from what I ate or due to emotions such as stress and anger. By learning more about eating healthily and cleansing my body of impurities, I also became a lot more sensitive to my energy levels. This enabled me to harness them.

Many of us who use our intellectual capacities to the maximum in our work operate solely from the mind, and this means, naturally, that the brain is always engaged. Many of us are so focused on this that we don't connect our brains to the rest of our bodies.

You can automatically tell how in tune you are with your body by the amount of physical tension you feel and the time it takes to develop. If you get a sharp headache or pain in your neck and shoulders, the likely cause is that you have ignored your body for quite some time, and now the signals are amplified to a point where you need to take notice. Your body will continue to increase the pain until you take action. Nothing really happens suddenly. Pain, tension and other symptoms of stress are your body's way of giving you feedback. You can eliminate most physical symptoms just by paying closer attention to them.

Body consciousness is the pathway to an increase in energy. The more you can sense the subtleties of stress and tension in your body, the more you can release them and let your natural energy flow.

Stress and tension are hindrances to your natural energy levels. They exhaust the body. Think of stress as your body working out all day but overtraining and using the wrong muscles. You still use energy, but the effect is destructive to the body, causing you to end up tired and in pain (we haven't even discussed the long-term effects). The more you develop a sense of body–mind consciousness, the more you can eliminate stress and tension and maximise your energy.

The additional benefits to your health include:

1 eliminating stress-related symptoms such as headaches;

2 detecting illnesses such as colds and flu; and

3 enabling you to take action to get rid of them.

Practising advanced breathing will help you improve your body awareness. It doesn't take long to do, and the more you do it, the better you will feel – mentally and physically.

Exercise: The check-in

This exercise is designed to check in and develop an increased sensitivity to your body.

1 While using gentle belly breathing, start noticing the sensations in your body. Start from one end of your

body and move your awareness to the other end of your body, one part at a time.

2 If you start at your feet, move your awareness to your calves, then up to your knees, thighs, pelvis, groin, buttocks and the muscles in your stomach, chest, back, shoulders, wrists, arms, hands, neck, throat, head, brain, eyes, ears, nose and mouth.

3 Pay particular attention to the areas in your head, such as your skull, scalp and the areas of your brain. See if you discover anything new.

Stress stores

As you practise the Check-in exercise, you will discover where you store your stress. This is where the muscles become tense. By paying attention to your 'stress stores', you can alleviate headaches, neck pain, migraines and other tension-related symptoms. Common areas of stress are in the face, such as the eyes, eyebrows, forehead and jaw. Stress areas are the scalp, the neck, throat, shoulders and back.

Exercise: Stress stores

1 Find your stress stores by paying particular attention to your back, shoulders, neck, head, scalp, forehead, temples and eyes. You don't need to do any work; just notice any tension you may feel. Don't resist it or try to get rid of it – just acknowledge it.

2 Now, wherever you feel pain, focus on it and try to relax the area, either by physically massaging it or by willing the body to relax. ▶

3 At first massage will be easier, but after some practice you will be able to release tension at will. With enough awareness you can concentrate on the individual muscles and relax them. It's like learning to raise one eyebrow; it just takes some practice to find and isolate the right muscles.

The one eyebrow principle

So far we have talked about relaxing muscles. Normally we have many muscles in the body that we cannot voluntarily relax. This is just because we haven't become sensitive enough to detect them. However you are capable, with practice, of isolating these muscles.

For example, if you've ever tried to raise one eyebrow while keeping the other still, you'll know that both eyebrows will rise together initially, because our brains aren't used to raising only one by itself. You'll have to practise for a while to isolate the muscles to keep one eyebrow in position and to raise the other. After some practice, however, your brain will activate the neural connections that allow it to raise one eyebrow by itself.

We apply this same principle to being able to tune in to specific muscles and relax them. Through using this technique I've been able to relax muscles in the head and face and even the muscles in the eyes. Mastering this has made a huge improvement in my eyesight. I've been slightly long-sighted and used to suffer from eyestrain and was unable to read for more than five minutes without glasses. Through becoming sensitive to my eye muscles and relaxing them, I can go several hours without my eyes feeling strained, and I hardly ever need to wear my glasses.

Another way to increase your body's sensitivity is to do a detox: it gives you a chance to rebalance your system. To do this: go on a three-day fruit diet, where all you eat is fruit. Buy a large variety of fruit so you don't get bored, but also make sure you eat enough to meet your energy requirements. If you get a headache or feel weak, this is a sign that you are not getting enough energy and need to eat more. Consult your doctor before starting if you have any medical condition.

During the detox you will develop a much greater sensitivity to your energy levels, as well as clearing out your system. Your body gives up addictions and instinctively finds what it needs. For example, after your detox, you may notice that you start to taste more subtle differences in food.

HARNESSING ENERGY

CASE STUDY

If you've ever taken a one-week vacation to go skiing or snowboarding, you may relate to this story. I love snowboarding and go once a year, at least. During the first two or three days, I am excited and full of energy, and I go for it at full pelt – I'll try anything. Then, around the fourth or fifth day, aches and pains start to affect my body, causing me to feel a bit tired. Now, because

▶

I love boarding, I keep going, demanding more from my body and getting up despite the aches and pains. I take additional precautions, such as making sure I get a good night's sleep and eating food that is easy to digest. By the end of the week, after I have pushed past the initial barrier, I find that my body has more energy and I want to continue being active. I demanded more energy from my body and worked to support it in having that energy.

Once you've developed some proficiency in body consciousness, you should start to notice your own energy levels a bit more. So, how do you get more energy from your body? You have to ask for it! There are few ways to ask for more energy.

You can just go hell for leather and exercise until your body gets used to the demands, or you can harness it by using breathing and meditative techniques. The former way is easy in principle but requires willpower and the right habits to make sure you don't overdo it.

For our purposes here, we will distinguish two types of energy: hard energy and soft energy.

HARD ENERGY

Hard energy is the energy of excitement and enthusiasm; of motion and emotion – the type of energy you experience when you are at a great concert or watching a football match (and your team is winning) or just plain sports or exercise. Your energy can be influenced by your surroundings, your emotions or your actions. And when you create hard energy you also increase the endorphins in your body. Endorphins are the chemicals produced in your brain that make you feel good, reduce pain and increase your immune system.

A good example of someone creating hard energy is Tony Robbins. At his seminars he is a master at energising the crowd by using exercises to make his audience feel positive and energised, such as getting everyone to give each other a high five or paying a compliment to the person sitting next to you.

It is quite easy to access hard energy. Exercises used to 'psyche yourself up', or mentally prepare you for some task, will do the trick. For example, when salespeople gear up for a sales call, they might walk around pumping their fists in the air, imagining being successful and making the sale.

To generate hard energy, you need to think of something exciting, and you will find yourself *becoming* excited. Move your body in a way that energises you. If you are not in the mood, just fake it until you make it. You can get great boosts of energy by using these exercises:

Exercises for instant energy

- **Jump up and down** with excitement. Just jump up and down and be excited for 30 seconds. If you're not in the mood, again just fake it until you make it. ▶

The more you practice this, the more proficient you will become. Practise being more excited than you have ever been. You may want to do this somewhere a bit private.

- **Energy clap**. A quick technique I do when I want to get ready for action. Just clap your hands together and shout (or think it to yourself) something like 'Let's go!', 'Let's rock' or 'I'm ready!' This doesn't generate as much energy as other exercises but it induces a mental shift to psyche you up for another activity or just to get cracking on what you are already doing.

- **The surprise technique**. A great way to wake up your body if you are feeling tired. While sitting nor-mally, suddenly imagine yourself being surprised by something that creates a shock to your system, like someone throwing ice-cold water in your face. Take in a sharp breath and really imagine it so that it seems real to you. Your imagination is so powerful that the brain can't tell the difference between imagination and reality (if you do it right). Allow your imagination to awaken you to alertness.

■ **Primal roar.** You'll need to do this where you can make some noise. Just let out a scream or a roar at the top of your voice. Pour any emotion you want into it. The idea is to let go and rip, tap into your primal nature. You'll instantly wake up and feel more alert.

■ **The fun factor.** Probably the simplest way to have more energy is to increase the amount of fun you have in your life. Have you noticed when you have more fun you feel more energetic and need less sleep? Laughing releases endorphins in your brain and makes you feel better. Increase the amount of fun you have, preferably with no or limited alcohol as too much negates the effects. Be spontaneous and be open to having fun everywhere.

SOFT ENERGY

While hard energy is generated when you're in a state of excitement, your body generates soft energy when it is relaxed. When you relax and release the tension in your body, there is less resistance or stress restricting your natural energy, which starts to flow through you.

You will tend to notice it at the end of the day when, in place of feeling worn out, you are more at ease and energised. You've increased your endurance by eliminating your natural energy losses.

Doing meditation, tai chi, yoga or qigong are great ways to access soft energy and the more you practise these kind of exercises the more energy you will have, and you will also become more sensitive to your energy levels.

From the Eastern point of view we are working with internal energy; if looked at from a Western viewpoint we can say we are working with imagination or even the placebo effect. The placebo effect is the effect observed when a pill that is effectively inert has a medical effect on the body because the patient and physician believes it will. So, for example, a starch pill cures a headache because the patient believes s/he is taking an aspirin. It doesn't matter which viewpoint you choose – whatever works for you. The human body responds to your thoughts and emotions.

Most of the time this happens quite automatically; for example, when you feel embarrassed your body naturally responds, blood flows to the cheeks, they become hot and you feel warmer. This automatic response can actually be harnessed, enabling you to direct energy to where it is needed in the body. Try it: imagine energy flowing to your eyes and you should notice that they feel better, more 'awake', or less strained. You may feel your muscles in your eyes and even feel the blood flow to your eyes increase.

You can also use your imagination to feel energy in your hands. To try it, close your eyes and imagine energy flowing to your hands, making your hands warmer. Now notice how warm your hands feel. Open your eyes and see if there is more blood flow in your hands. Some of these sensations will take time so don't worry if it doesn't happen straight away, use the remaining exercises in this book to build up the relevant brain experiences.

Chi exercises

Chi flow

If during the breathing exercises you noticed the sensation of breathing beyond the physical capacity of your lungs, you'll have experienced some of what we are about to do next. If not, this exercise will train you.

1 Begin by doing the deep-breathing exercises.

2 Now, become aware of your body. Wherever you have tension, imagine yourself breathing into that area. Imagine a channel opening up from your lungs to the tense area so that each time you breathe, your breath (or chi energy) will be directed there. Put another way, imagine that you can breathe all the way into the affected area and allow the breath to travel there.

3 As the breath comes to this area, let the body part relax and allow the chi to flow into the area, energising it. ▶

4 This is a good technique for getting rid of light pain in the body and great for headaches. If you feel faint, return to normal breathing.

The dead possum technique

This is a good way to continue developing body sensitivity but also to energise the whole body at the same time.

1 Stop breathing for 10 seconds. Don't hold your breath – just stop breathing. Think of yourself as an actor, 'playing dead'.

2 Let go of all muscle sensations and all tension.

3 Notice your body starting to relax and that this relaxation becomes more profound.

4 Keeping this sense of relaxation, resume your breathing, isolating your lungs so that only the muscles needed for breathing are working and your other muscles are relaxed.

5 Now, when you breathe, maintain this sense of deep relaxation as you inhale and exhale.

6 Each time you inhale and get to the 'top' of your breath, allow your body to experience that 'letting go' sensation even more. You may even feel as though your body starts to expand when you breathe in. When you exhale and empty your lungs, allow your body to have the same sensation again.

7 With practice, you will get a deeper sense of relaxation.

Summary

We've just covered really powerful ways to energise the body. Remember it's a journey: so practise the exercises.

The Energy Equation: Energy = Peak physical energy minus Stress

Peak physical energy can be increased by:

1 Eating well.

2 Physical exercise.

3 Adequate sleep.

4 Having positive emotions.

There are three steps to reducing stress and allowing energy to flow.

1 Go from basic breathing to advanced breathing. Breathing is the foundation for relaxing the body.

2 Increase bodily awareness.

3 Tune in and relax.

Bodily awareness enables stress-related tension to be detected quickly, thus eliminating stress at its onset. Practising body consciousness also enables energy to be maximised.

Once we are relaxed our natural energy flows and can be directed to the areas that need it.

There are two types of energy. Hard energy is the energy of excitement and enthusiasm. Soft energy is the energy of relaxation.

Next, we will examine ways to eliminate stress by performing the body consciousness exercises that we have already started, to put you in even better shape.

CHAPTER 3

Into the resistance – letting go of stress

CASE STUDY

It is 11pm. I'm working on this complex financial model; there are about 20 Excel work sheets; I'm exhausted but also awake and wired. I've been drinking coffee and diet coke all day and my nerves feel frazzled. I've had on average 4.5 hours' sleep for the past two weeks. The model doesn't work, there's an error in it but I can't find it. I can barely even look at the screen, it's all becoming a jumble and my eyes and head hurt.

I've been working since 8.30am on the same Excel model with about 40 minutes' break all day. I've probably got two hours of work still to do once I fix this error, but I've been trying to fix it for the past hour. If I could think straight I'd probably do it in about 15 minutes but my mind is failing me. I bite the bullet, print out the spreadsheet and struggle on at what feels like half a mile per hour.

▶

Eventually I fix the model, go home and get to bed around 2am. Damn! Only five hours' potential sleep. I need to be up for 7. So I climb into bed, head on the pillow... And then... I can't sleep.

My mind keeps worrying. I left with 90% of the work done. The other 10% should take an hour, but what if there's an undetected mistake? What if some emergency happens and then I can't finish by my deadline? I didn't have time to do a sense check of the workings and give it a strategic look. I've just done the minimal and was too tired to engage my brain and look at the bigger picture.

I drift in and out of sleep and by the time I actually fall asleep properly, the alarm goes off. It feels like I've only had 10 minutes of sleep. I rush out of bed, shower, get ready, skip breakfast (I'll grab something later) and leave to make it into the office. I'm tired from lack of sleep and stress; my nerves are frazzled. I feel far from my best but nervous energy is propelling me forward. I manage to meet my deadline for the Excel model but there is still the second project. More work piles on and it seems to take me twice as long to get through anything. I'm just cranking out numbers; I'm not providing any critical insight.

Stress is an all-too-familiar companion in our lives. The story above illustrates a particularly difficult time I had at work at the beginning of my career. This stress cycle lasted for about three weeks, during which time I slept badly and the combination of fatigue and anxiety really affected my performance. I started making silly mistakes which cost me time and added to my anxiety. I could not see the wood for the trees and I ended up just doing, not *thinking*. The result was that both my performance and productivity went down noticeably to the point that the best thing to do was to leave before I got fired. Luckily, as we saw earlier, I got a transfer to a new department and was able to turn things around.

Hopefully you won't have experienced stress at this level, although I suspect many of you will. But it is a key factor in the working world and one that it is vital to understand and take control of.

There are generally two types of stressful situations we encounter in our non-life-threatening workplace (the other kinds of stressful situations are when you are being mugged on the street by a gang of thieves).

Stressful situation one arises from an immediate stressor, such as rushing around trying to fit two hours of work into an hour in order to meet an urgent deadline, or battling to make the commute to work on time, when there are transport delays and huge queues conspiring to stop you. At such times a stressor – deadline – causes your heart to pump faster and your body to produce adrenaline to 'get you going'.

Stressful situation two is creeping stress: though you can't physically see the stressor, you can feel it nonetheless; it is a slower, impending worry, rather than an immediate deadline. This can be caused by things like uncertainty about the future. For example, your firm announces there's a round of job cuts that will happen in the next few weeks; immediately this concern will be with you in the background.

Whether you are at your desk, lying in bed, or talking to a friend the uncertainty about your job security will put you in a state of worry and anxiety. In this case, you are antici-pating a future stressful event that you will need to resolve. The body still produces stress hormones, pumping your heart harder, even when you are not really doing anything.

We know that stress isn't good for us, but most of us feel helpless to do anything about our stress levels other than the occasional massage or yoga class at the end of the week … or a stiff drink or two.

A BRIEF HISTORY OF STRESS

Stress occurs when the brain's survival response mechanism takes over. As human beings we are naturally wired for survival, this has been in our makeup for millennia; your survival instinct is hard-wired into your brain.

When you are stressed the 'fight-or-flight' part of your brain signals danger. Even though we no longer live in the wild, we are automatically programmed to run from a deadly lion or rampaging herd of wild bulls. This is just as well, as we still need this reflex. If we needed to decide each time whether we should run or fight (as would be the case if the higher brain functions were in control), we would lose valuable seconds.

The primal part of our brain is there to protect us from danger by reacting immediately. When in 'fight-or-flight' mode, the body directs all of your resources into emergency functions. Heart rate and blood pressure increase; blood flow to the digestive organs is reduced, while that to the extremities increases so that you are ready for action. Glucose is sent into your bloodstream, while hormones are released to produce a rush of energy. The mid-brain is more active and you become alert and are able to react to the danger as it arrives.

Non-emergency functions, as viewed from the brain's survival perspective, are those bodily functions we can do without, while we either escape impending danger or batter our opponent. Non-emergency functions include digestion, immune system, cell repair and recovery, and higher brain functions such as critical thinking.

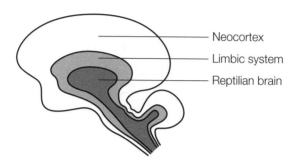

THE PARTS OF THE HUMAN BRAIN

These changes in our system enable us to fight or run away. In the Stone Age, such natural defences were essential, especially when our ancestors were in mortal danger. However, these instances of stress were of short duration.

The fight-or-flight reflexes are less useful today when the stress we feel is not in direct response to any 'real' danger. However the body still responds in the same way to stressful situations because our brain's natural instinct is to survive. However, we can unconsciously trigger stress when we think of past events and anticipate future ones. The brain still processes modern stresses as life-threatening; psychological and emotional threats get the same treatment as physical ones. It is our ego or sense of self that is under threat most of the time. We will examine this later in the chapter.

A little stress is not a bad thing – the body restores itself over time. However, we were not designed for continual stress. We need those non-emergency functions and when they are depleted over time, as when we have chronic stress, it has serious impacts on our health.

THE DAMAGING EFFECTS OF STRESS

Let's examine in more detail some of the effects of long-term stress:

1 Your heart pumps faster, directing blood to the limbs and causing blood pressure to increase. This is fine on a short-term basis, but over time your heart stays at an accelerated rate, maintaining high blood pressure.

2 Your rate of breathing increases.

3 Blood sugar levels increase as the output of the pancreas and liver and the storage mechanism of fat cells change. Increasing blood sugar lowers insulin levels. This can lead to adult diabetes.

4 The digestive system is compromised as the blood moves away from the intestines to the extremities. Internal organs don't regenerate as effectively. Even if you have a healthy diet, when the body is stressed digestion is impaired.

5 Higher brain functions, in the neocortex, are diminished as your thinking shifts to the reptilian brain (which controls our primal instincts), affecting your reasoning capabilities. This is why it feels harder to think straight. Goodbye critical thinking and creativity.

6 Adrenalin and cortisol are produced, ready for action, but when we are stationary they don't get used, causing hypertension.

7 Unused adrenalin and cortisol in the tissues cause muscles to tighten, contract and feel sore.

8 These chemicals also impair sleep so the body does not regenerate properly.

9 Your immune system becomes compromised, leaving you more susceptible to illness or disease. We are more likely to get colds and flu when stressed.

10 Less cellular repair occurs, which could cause you to age prematurely.

11 Other non-urgent functions are diminished, which can lead to lack of libido, or impotence. So it has a big impact on sex life and relationships.

When we do not deal with stress, we live in a stressful state all the time. This produces long-term damage in the body, depleting the resources needed for repair and regeneration. In addition, the chemicals produced by stress such as adrenalin and glucocortisoids can cause cellular breakdown. No wonder we feel tired when we are stressed!

When you are switched on to long-term stress your brain remains on red or yellow alert; you are constantly monitoring your environment for threats, and this can make you paranoid, defensive or aggressive.

Imagine if you were trekking through one of the deadliest jungles in the world. In this jungle it is reputed that some of the most dangerous creatures live. There are poisonous snakes in the undergrowth, large pythons that could drop down from the trees, ferocious jaguars hiding up in the tree tops, leeches hiding in pools of water that will stick to you and suck your blood.

In this situation, even though there is no current stressor, there is the threat of an impending one, so you would be on constant alert, your mind on constant lookout and ready for the worst. This in turn would mean that your senses would be hypervigilant, your heart would be pumping and you would be ready for action – to run as soon as you saw something dangerous. By the time you reached camp at the end of the day you would be exhausted, worn out by the constant feeling of dread.

This is exactly the mode that our brain is operating in when we are working in stressful situations. Hopefully there are no poisonous snakes in your office, or at least only metaphorical ones. The threats are different in nature; they are more based on the survival of the ego and our emotional or financial security than our physical body. But the response is the same, we are on constant alert for any mistakes that would make us look incompetent, upset our immediate bosses, make our customers dissatisfied, anything that would ultimately cost us our jobs. You have already calculated in your mind the worst-case scenario, which is being fired, losing your job, having a bad reputation. These in turn will result in you ending up broke, losing your house, not being able to support yourself, your family and your lifestyle, and ultimately failure. This is a common fear that lurks as the big bogey man for many high achievers.

So with all this worry going on in the background it is little surprise that we can often feel stressed and exhausted at the end of the day.

THE STRESS LOOP

When we get stressed we develop the physical symptoms mentioned previously. These cause more psychological stress (as we get stressed about our symptoms) which increases our physical symptoms and so on. We get caught in a negative spiral of increasing stress and decreasing wellbeing.

This is why chronic stress is so dangerous to our health. With all those symptoms going on, we lose sleep, we weaken our immune system and digestion and allow colds, flu and more serious diseases to take effect. (Though actually, going down with the flu can work out if it forces us to stop and relax!)

As well as the physical effects of the stress loop, after some time our bodies become desensitised to the stress biochemicals they produce. The more stressed you become, the harder it is to turn off the mechanism. It becomes normal to operate at a particular level of stress so you don't notice it. However, you will still have the same physical symptoms. Think of the number of people who live with an elevated blood pressure, aches and pains and frequent indigestion as if it were normal. After all a trip to the pharmacy to get some medication will take care of those symptoms.

STRESS WARNING SIGNS

How can you tell when you are stressed? If you suffer from mild stress, it will be obvious, but if you are experiencing long-term stress, you may not even notice it. Here are some warning signs:

■ Inability to think clearly.

■ Emotional distress, fatigue or numbness.

■ Repetitively worrying about the same things.

■ Feeling tired a great deal.

■ Experiencing constant aches and pains.

■ Increase in addictive behaviours such as smoking, drinking.

■ Repeated illnesses like colds, flu and backache.

Through practising body consciousness exercises (Chapter 2), you will start to detect stress a lot earlier as symptoms you may have been desensitised to become more apparent. In addition you will be able to start eliminating stress.

HOW DO PEOPLE NORMALLY DEAL WITH STRESS?

Most people think they are good at dealing with stress, but really they are only good at managing or suppressing the immediate symptoms. They ignore it (until it gets too great), find a quick release, sublimate it or, worse, they allow it to build up like a pressure cooker, with negative consequences.

In my experience, even when they know they are stressed the most common reaction from people is a variant of 'if I can just get past this point then the stress will be over'. It usually sounds like: 'I'll just hang on until my vacation in a few weeks' time' or 'If I can just get through till after reporting period then it will be OK', or 'This is just a tough week it will be fine next week'.

Some of the common ways of coping with stress are cigarettes, alcohol, drugs, sex, avoidance and procrastination, going on vacation or living till the weekend. When we begin to use these activities as coping mechanisms, we are not dealing with the problem – we are merely masking it. Anything that creates a high can be used to temporarily deal with stress. That's why cigarettes, drugs and sex work. Unfortunately they can become addictions. The problem with these mechanisms is that the stress might be relieved temporarily but they never solve the underlying problem.

Alcohol

Many people turn to alcohol to reduce stress, which is fine in moderation and under normal circumstances. Alcohol definitely makes most people feel better temporarily. However, it also increases blood sugar levels and hinders the body's absorption of vitamin B and zinc, which are nutrients that help keep us calm. Invariably, the 'high' we feel while drinking alcohol is followed by a 'low' of lethargy when our blood sugar drops to low levels. Low blood sugar prevents us from getting a good night's sleep. In addition alcohol is a sort of 'poison' to the body so your body needs to work to eliminate it

Vacations

Everyone loves vacations. They are certainly great opportunities to unwind, but many people will go for weeks at a time, accumulating stress, with the promise of a vacation in the future. This is fine if you go every weekend and if the thought of a vacation actually relaxes your mind. But if you are subjecting yourself to stress for weeks at a time, with the promise of a vacation as your reward for all the hard work you're putting in, then you are sacrificing your long-term health for the sake of a week or so of relaxation.

Your body may get some temporary relief and start to recover during your time off, but a week of recovery won't make up for weeks of stress. In addition, by the time you get back to work, your job seems even worse than before and you're straight back into the stress. If you live in the 'I can't wait to go on holiday' or 'I'll feel much better after my next vacation' mode then it is time to start looking at the stress in your current situation. It is time to implement stress elimination techniques. They'll be much cheaper and you'll be able to enjoy every day, not just those two weeks in August.

Procrastination

This is a huge problem for many. Procrastinating provides temporary relief to stress, a respite from the stressful feelings, only to have them come back in profusion as there is now less time to deal with the issue that is causing the stress. The stress–procrastination loop becomes an addictive pattern. The brain gets the same effect as from a chemical addiction.

BREAKING THE STRESS–RELIEF CYCLE

If you find yourself in the same pattern of stress and relief, these habits are part of your stress cycle. They enable you to cope by giving you a temporary fix, but never provide you with any true freedom from stress. Some people go for years in this cycle; but at the cost of broken relationships, missed opportunities at work, impaired wellbeing and a lot of time wasted. This cycle can be broken. I know people who have been trapped for years but regain control of their lives after breaking out of the cycle.

So how do we break out of the stress loop when we are in the thick of it? The first step is to remove ourselves from the stressor. Going for a walk or doing some kind of exercise is a natural way to relieve ourselves of this stress loop. However, it is important that we don't pick up where we left off when we return! Deep breathing and other forms of relaxation clear the mind. When you are relaxed, you feel more creative, and a creative mind-set is often the best way to deal with problems. You want to engage your mind so you can notice the loop and choose another way.

Then it's time to get to know your stress triggers. The more you can recognise what stresses you, the easier it is to eliminate it.

Almost all stress triggers are really threats to the ego, self. For example, one of my stress triggers is the fear of making a mistake, and even worse being caught publicly making a mistake. Even though intellectually I know it is OK to make mistakes, I'm instantly thrown back to something in my childhood at school where making a mistake meant embarrassment. It is my ego that is under threat here, not my life, but the brain doesn't make the distinction between the two very well. Most triggers will be around the fear of the loss of something – reputation, control, admiration and trust are common.

THE TOP 10 CAUSES OF STRESS ARE:

1 Childhood trauma

2 Death of a loved one

3 Divorce

4 Finances

5 Employment

6 Health

7 Personal relationships

8 Chronically ill child

9 Pregnancy

10 Danger, i.e. any hazardous event that is out of the ordinary for an individual

The American Institute of Stress

Exercise: Identifying stress

Answer the following questions to identify your stress triggers:

1 What triggers stress for you? What type of situation? When stressed, look at what you are trying to prevent happening.

2 How does stress 'show itself' in your lifestyle? How do you respond to stress – in what ways? (See the box below for some examples.)

3 What emotions do you experience when you are stressed?

▶

4 What thoughts go through your mind when you are stressed?

5 What are the physical symptoms of stress?

6 Where do you store your stress?

7 What methods do you use to cope with stress?

8 How long do you stay in a state of stress?

EXAMPLES OF FEELINGS AND STATES ASSOCIATED WITH STRESS:

- Frustration
- Cravings for food cigarettes, drugs
- Nothing seems to be working
- Clumsiness
- Irritated by small things, feeling snappy, aggressive
- Feeling 'checked out'
- Can't seem to relax, things lurk in the back of the mind
- Cloudiness in the head
- Overwhelmed
- Excessive 'busyness'
- Can't see the forest for the trees
- In constant 'go' mode – have to be doing something, even if it is not productive
- Feeling like you are running on a treadmill and going nowhere

WHAT TO DO WHEN YOU'RE IN THE THICK OF IT

When you're in the midst of a stressful situation the chances are it may take some time to recognise that you're stressed in the first place and then to calm your mind down. Here are some exercises to bring an immediate stop to stress.

Exercises for dealing with stress

Stop and listen approach

1 As soon as you notice yourself being stressed, just stop what you are doing.

2 Acknowledge that you are feeling stressed and don't allow yourself to become more 'stressed about being stressed'. That's very common but counterproductive.

3 Ask yourself, 'What is the underlying fear that is causing this stress?' Usually when we are stressed there is an unconscious fear underneath. See the box for common fears. For example, I might screw this up and look bad or get fired. My boss or colleagues may not like me.

4 Is this a rational fear? Are you blowing the consequences out of proportion?

5 Look at the worst-case scenario: 'Would I survive?'

6 Now look at the most likely scenario: what do you need to do to resolve the situation and let it go? When you've resolved it then let it go.

COMMON FEARS AT THE SOURCE OF STRESS

- Loss of love
- Loss of status
- Loss of control
- Fear of making a mistake
- Fear of not being capable
- Fear of not being worthy
- Being alone

Other exercises

- Be present – begin to bring your awareness to the present moment. To do this, cycle through your five senses. Notice what you see; use your peripheral vision so you can take in more. What do you hear? What can you smell? What do you feel on your skin? What can you taste? Continue for about five minutes or until you feel calmer.

- Do exercises to promote energy (see Chapter 2).

- Perform the 'Nothingness meditation'. Go somewhere quiet where you can sit or lie down for 20 to 30 minutes, undisturbed. During that time, do absolutely nothing. Mentally tell yourself that there is nothing you need to do right now. Repeat this in your mind as a mantra and continue to allow yourself to relax.

EUSTRESS

CASE STUDY

The other day I was on an amazing three-day business course. The event was a lot of fun. I had a blast. We were put through some stressful situations and it brought out my driven competitive nature. On the last day I was inspired and wired. I went home ready to put it all into practice. I did some work that night and for the next few days I felt happy, inspired, creative and charged up.

I couldn't sit still. I had to keep working and getting the new ideas out. Yes this was fantastic, but I noticed after the second day I felt constantly 'wired'. My heart rate was faster than normal, as was my pulse; my body felt a bit tense and I could not calm down even when I was doing nothing. I didn't sleep much and didn't feel the need for much sleep.

After a while I became a bit concerned as I could see the danger of being 'wired' is exactly the same as that of being stressed a lot, so I took time out to calm down my body.

It actually took a long time to calm my body down. Taking long deep breaths, which usually calm the body, didn't work. So I had to try something new.

So-called positive stress, eustress, can be a great thing. You feel good, you're in action and it feels a lot better than negative stress. There is a feeling of excitement. While it feels great, unfortunately, just like negative stress, too much eustress can be bad for your health. In the primitive man this would be the fight response instead of the flight response. He would probably have been hunting a wild animal and been close to making a kill. He would have been excited at the possibility of succeeding and needed that extra push, the extra alertness, more power to the legs, quicker reaction time, and his body would give it to him by going into the stress state. Back in the modern world the success is usually further off and more abstract but it feels like you need to chase after it, hence the fight response becomes useful. Even though you feel good you are still triggering the same mechanism for negative stress and you will still have a faster heart rate, higher blood pressure, reduced digestion, etc. So after a prolonged period of eustress (any more than a day) it is a good idea to calm the body down.

Reducing eustress

This is a good exercise for dealing with eustress (which can also work with anxiety). We have more control over our automatic nervous system than we think and by using this principle we are going to slow down our heart rate back to normal. The trick is to talk to your body. That's right: talk to your body. Tell it to calm down. After a while it will respond. You don't have to verbally talk, just mentally talk.

1 Start off by breathing deeply into the abdomen, hold-ing the breath for a couple of seconds on the inhale

and exhale. When holding your breath, allow your body to relax.

2 Now tell your body to calm down and imagine that it does. Put your hand on your heart and say, 'It is OK, you can calm down now.'

3 Imagine your heart rate slowing and going back to normal, with your breathing. Tell yourself there is nothing you need to do right now except relax. You will still reach your goals.

4 If you are so inclined, imagine your mind as the parent and your body as the child. Speak to your body as you would a child, being reassuring, caring but in control.

5 After five minutes or so of doing this you should notice a significant improvement.

You can use this technique with any heightened emotional state. I have taught this to my coaching clients. It worked particularly well with a woman who was experiencing heightened emotional distress and kept crying uncontrollably for several days. I taught her this technique and she found she could calm her crying outbreaks.

Exercise: The de-stress technique

We've looked at some urgent stress release techniques for when you are in the thick of it. But what about the more general need to wind down after work? Rather than reach for a glass of wine or the remote control, ▶

here is an exercise to enable you to quickly leave work behind at the end of the day and free your mind of any worries about it. Then you can use your evening or weekend to fully relax, unwind and refresh. It's a highly effective way to get rid of stress and particularly useful if you feel overwhelmed or have too much going on.

This is a written exercise, but you can also do it with a partner. It will help clear out some of the background thoughts and unresolved issues which run in the back of your mind and keep you stressed, helping you be in the present moment.

1 Begin by getting a pad and a pen.

2 We will do a simple 'brain dump'. Just write down everything that is on your mind right now.

3 Use these prompts to help you with your thinking:

- All the things that you need to do.

- Any worries or any concerns that you are experiencing.

- Any people you need to speak to.

- Any problems or challenges that you're facing.

- Anything you need to remember.

- Anything that you said you would do and haven't done yet.

- Anyone you're annoyed with.

4 Just keep writing, don't stop until you've written every-thing down. You'll know when you're done: when you feel there is nothing more to write.

Once you've written everything down look over the list and select or highlight the things on the list that are important to you. We will filter those into two categories.

- Category 1 are the things that you can do something about.

- Category 2 are those that you feel that you can't do anything about right now. There's no obvious solution or the solution is out of your hands.

5 Take a clean sheet of paper; draw a line down the centre of the page to make two columns.

6 With category 1, those items that you can do something about, write down the actions that you need to take to resolve those situations in the category 1 column. Examples: people you need to speak to, actions you need to take, things you need to work out, any research you need to do or get done, and so forth. If the next actions are obvious, then you may not need to write them down, just write down the item.

7 For category 2 items, the things that you can't do anything about, we want to turn those problems into questions. When you turn a problem that seems unresolvable into a question, you gear your mind up for dealing with it. For each category 2 item, write down a question that if you had the answer to it the problem would be resolved.

8 You may come up with a solution by yourself or you might find it by speaking to someone. Generally the easiest way to resolve your questions is to ask someone who can help. Now think of someone that you ▶

can speak to about this issue. This could be a friend; it could be a work colleague; someone you can confide in, could be a coach, doctor or therapist.

9 Now that you have category 1s and category 2s, schedule to complete each item, or schedule some time in your diary to go through your list and deal with each item.

10 Now that you've written everything down that's bothering you and scheduled when you're going to handle them you can let go of them for now – decide that you're no longer going to worry because everything you have to do is scheduled to be resolved at an appropriate time, so there's nothing left to worry about.

CHAPTER 4

Super sleep

If you ask most people how much sleep we should get, the common answer will be eight hours. This is a generally established paradigm accepted by most people, but the 'eight hours a night' was established relatively recently in our society, mostly in response to the industrial revolution and workers' needs for regulation.

In other cultures, sleep patterns vary. The traditional Mediterranean sleep profile is five hours a night with an hour's nap in the middle of the day. The Masai tribe in Africa only sleep three to four hours a night. Many ancient societies had two sleeping 'shifts' during the night, separated by several hours of wakefulness.

A study recently suggested that insomnia may be a result of the sufferers' bodies being attuned to our ancient sleeping habit of four hours' sleep, followed by a couple of hours of wakefulness and then another four hours' sleep.

In addition, people have experimented with other sleeping patterns, such as extreme napping habits, known as polyphasic sleep – sleeping 20–30 minutes every four to six hours. This demonstrates that it is possible to live on two to six hours of sleep per day over an extended period.

In Western society many successful people have lived on less than eight hours' sleep – Margaret Thatcher only slept five hours each night; Napoleon slept only four hours. More interestingly, people have done temporary stints of polyphasic sleeping which involve replacing a nighttime sleep with naps of 20–30 minutes in a set pattern. Proponents of this include Henry Ford, Benjamin Franklin and Thomas Jefferson.

The Scientist Buckminster Fuller followed a polyphasic sleeping pattern, sleeping 20–30 minutes every six hours, which he continued for two years. Steve Pavlina writes an interesting blog on polyphasic sleep, which is worth a read: check out **www.stevepavlina.com**.

There is a lot of conflicting research about what constitutes the 'best' length of sleep. For example a six-year study (*Archives of General Psychiatry*, February 2002, Vol. 59, No. 2) conducted by Kripke of more than a million adults from the ages of 30 to 102 revealed that people who get only six to seven hours of sleep at night have a lower death rate than those who get eight hours' sleep or more. This suggests that six to seven hours of sleep is a more ideal time span.

But, for our purposes right now, we are interested in getting the right sleep to enable you to have maximum energy to achieve more in your waking hours.

WHY DO WE NEED SLEEP?

Sleep is essential to maintain a healthy immune system and allow the body to repair itself. The cells in the body regenerate throughout the day but during sleep the body can concentrate all of its resources on repair. Sleep also enables the brain to maintain normal levels of cognitive skills such as speech, memory and innovative and flexible thinking. When we suffer from lack of sleep, we become groggy, find it difficult to concentrate and become irritable. If we are deprived of sleep for more than a day our bodies will eventually force a shut down – you will not be able to resist sleep, taking micro naps if necessary.

HOW WE SLEEP – THE SLEEP CYCLE

Let's look at how sleep occurs during the night. It is regulated by an internal body clock. Sleep goes in cycles throughout the night, moving back and forth between deep, restorative sleep, more alert stages and dreaming. Each cycle lasts approximately 90 minutes, with the deepest sleep occurring in the first or second phase. As sleep progresses, deep sleep periods become shorter, and more time is spent in dream (or lighter) sleep.

There are two main types of sleep:

■ REM (Rapid Eye Movement) sleep is when we dream most actively. During REM, our eyes move back and forth, as we are 'dreaming in pictures'.

■ Non-REM (NREM) sleep consists of four stages of deeper
   and deeper sleep. Each sleep stage is important for the
   overall quality of sleep, but deep sleep and REM sleep are
   especially vital to the system.

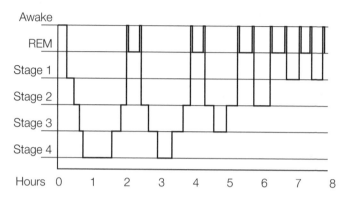

THE SLEEP CYCLE

Non-REM sleep is divided into four stages:

Stage 1 (drowsiness) – The brain is in the alpha state: the
same state we would have if we meditated or closed our
eyes for a few minutes. Stage 1 lasts 5–10 minutes. The
eyes move slowly under the eyelids, muscle activity slows
down and we are easily awakened.

Stage 2 (light sleep) – This stage lasts for approximately
20 minutes. Eye movements stop, the heart rate slows
and the body temperature decreases. If you take a nap,
do not go beyond this stage otherwise you will feel groggy
upon waking.

Stage 3 (deep sleep) – This is a transitional period between
light sleep and very deep sleep. Brain activity moves to
the delta state.

Stage 4 (delta sleep) – This stage is referred to as delta sleep because of the slow brain wave activity. We're difficult to awaken, and if we are awakened, we do not adjust immediately and often feel groggy and disoriented for several minutes.

REM sleep (dream sleep) – Once we have gone from stage 1 through to stage 4, we then cycle back up and experience our first REM sleep, about 70 to 90 minutes into the sleep cycle. We usually have three to five REM episodes per night. This stage is associated with processing emotions, retaining memories and relieving stress.

The deepest sleep occurs most often in the earliest hours of a night's sleep. In fact, we complete most of our deep, restorative sleep in the first four hours. Much of the fifth hour of sleep is REM sleep, which is psychologically beneficial in that it keeps us in a good mood. At the end of the fifth hour of sleep, we will probably not sleep any more deeply than stage 2, which explains why people who sleep less than eight hours can still get a good night's sleep.

In fact, when we sleep too much, our sleep stages are distributed over a wider period of time. You may have difficulty getting to sleep or take longer to fall asleep. Conversely, it has been shown that when people are used to shortened sleep periods, they fall into deep sleep and REM more rapidly and experience more efficient sleep.

Sleep research is a bit contradictory. A great deal of research suggests that eight hours is a must, but other research concludes that it is fine to get less than eight hours and even advocates sleeping for only six to seven hours. Given this contradictory research, I always come back to working with what is best for the individual. However, the first thing is to release the psychological brakes that say you need eight hours' sleep. I want you to be open-minded and try out sleeping less. If you are ill or recovering from illness you may need more than the minimum.

Experiment by reducing your sleep to six or seven hours for a three-week period to determine if this works for you. When experimenting expect it to work, or at least allow it to challenge what you already know. Many people's beliefs about how much sleep they need really makes the difference. When people believe that something will not work, usually they are right. When people try something with the intention of making it work, or to challenge what they know, they are usually pleasantly surprised.

Personally, since reducing my sleep time, I go through phases during which I am so motivated that I see sleep as a waste of time, and while in this state I sleep less than five to six hours a night. Other times, I go back to my standard seven hours. My initial barrier to sleeping less was the worry that I would look haggard, so I was insistent on eight hours because I thought I needed it for optimal health. Since I challenged these beliefs, I don't look any more haggard than when I was sleeping eight hours a night. The only time I get eight hours or more is when fighting off an impending cold or flu or after a heavy gym workout when my body feels as if it needs to recover. Other than for those factors I rarely go over eight hours. Even at the weekends.

GETTING QUALITY SLEEP

Given the debate on how much sleep we need, let's focus on the quality, not the quantity. Here are the key factors to getting quality sleep.

Relaxation

The main factor preventing quality sleep is going to bed when either your mind is too busy or your body is not relaxed. Anything that stimulates mental activity, such as worrying, watching an intense film or surfing the net can put your brain into a highly active state which is not conducive to a good night's rest.

If you find yourself tossing and turning at night it's a sure sign you have pent-up energy which needs to be released and that you won't be fully benefiting from sleep. Doing simple stretches or yoga exercises is a good way to release this stressful energy. There are exercises later in this chapter which will show you how.

If, on the other hand, you can get into bed fully relaxed, you are giving your body and mind the best conditions in which to restore and repair and gain the most from the time asleep.

Time

As we've already discussed, six to eight hours of sleep is adequate; experiment with the number of hours that work for you.

Lifestyle

Live a lifestyle that supports or compensates for the number of hours you sleep – make sure you are eating healthily, getting some regular exercise and have a consistent sleep schedule as much as possible.

Preparation for a good night's sleep

- **Minimise coffee intake before bed**. Don't have coffee within four hours of going to bed. If you find it difficult to fall asleep at night, you should cut back on caffeine altogether because you may feel its effects hours after you consume it.

- **Minimise alcohol**. Alcohol can certainly make you feel relaxed, but too much of it will disturb your sleep patterns. You'll feel sleepy initially but it will prevent you from going into a deep, relaxing sleep.

- **Go to sleep with a clear head**. If you take your worries to bed, your mind will stay in the alpha zone and won't be able to descend into the delta state. Remember, not getting enough sleep won't kill you, but worrying about it will compound the feeling of tiredness. The exercises later in this chapter will help you relax your mind before sleep. If you wake up with worries on your mind, a quick jotting down of all the things bothering you allows you to get enough stuff out of your head so you can relax. (See the de-stress exercise in Chapter 3).

- **Avoid working or surfing the web just before bed**. Working and surfing the internet may keep your mind in a highly active state, and make it difficult to go to sleep. You want your brain to go from active to relaxed.

■ **Avoid sleeping pills**. These may cause you to fall asleep, but they can keep you from getting the deep sleep you need to feel truly rested. You may also become dependent on sleeping pills, physiologically or psychologically, depending on the kind of tablets you take.

■ **Don't exercise just before bed**. Exercising from one to two hours before bedtime acts as a stimulant and tends to raise your body temperature. This is fine if you want to stay awake, but if you want to fall asleep quickly, confine exercise to the morning, afternoon or early evening. Gentle exercise such as yoga, however, is a great way to send the body to sleep because you get rid of any tension and nervous energy you may have.

■ **Go to bed when you are tired**. Trying to sleep when you are not tired is not only a waste of time but you can often weaken the association your mind has with bed and sleep. You want to go to bed when tired so that you can fall asleep quickly. This forms an association in your subconscious mind of bed and sleep. Doing other activities in bed such as watching TV can make it harder to fall asleep straight away as your mind associates other activities with bed.

■ **Create a winding down routine**. If you find it hard to get ready to sleep, create a routine to calm you down and prepare you for bed. Take a warm bath or shower, darken the room, put candles on instead of lights. Playing calming music will relax you and get you to wind down.

Exercise for relaxation before sleeping

This exercise helps you to relax your body before sleeping. It works by relaxing each part of the body in turn, giving a total body relaxation.

1 Lie in bed in a comfortable position.

2 Start with your legs. Tense all the muscles in your legs including your feet. Hold for five seconds then let go and relax. Feel the tension completely drain away as you relax.

3 Then do the same with your torso, including stomach muscles, back and chest.

4 Then tense all the muscles in your arms, including your hands, for five seconds and relax.

5 Finally, tense the muscles in your neck, face and head and relax.

6 Feel the relaxation that you now have as you let the tension go.

HOW TO DEAL WITH BOUTS OF INSOMNIA

A symptom of stress, occasional insomnia can strike us all. There are many things which can cause insomnia. The following techniques are for occasional insomnia that is not caused by a medical condition. For persistent insomnia I recommend seeing a doctor. If you find yourself waking up in the night and you can't get back to sleep the likely causes are physical restlessness, stress or mental overstimulation (for example having a genius idea in the middle of the night).

Pent-up energy

When the body is restless there is pent-up energy needing to be released. The problem is that doing any exercise is going to wake you up. The trick is to release the energy in the place where it feels pent-up. This is often in the back and the legs. The best method for this is stretching. The following two stretches are the most useful and ones you can do in bed.

For physical tension

Star stretch

You know when you wake up in the morning, yawn and then stretch? You are releasing the morning tension. Well if you do it at night you will also release any tension.

1 Simply lie on your back and stretch your arms and legs out as far and as much as comfortably possible and let the tension and energy drain away. You should feel a release of energy.

Cat stretch

The star stretch worked on the limbs. The cat stretch works on the back:

1 Kneel on all fours, knees under hips, hands under shoulders.

2 Take a deep breath. As you exhale, arch your back towards the ceiling, stretching the back.

3 Come back to centre and arch your back the other way. Repeat.

Take it easy at first to warm up and then stretch as much as is comfortable.

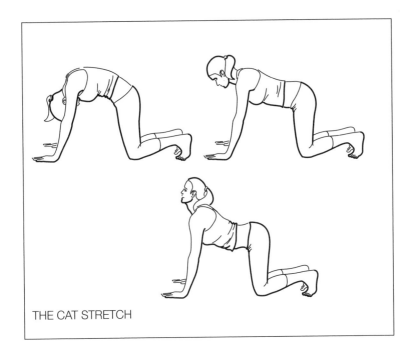

THE CAT STRETCH

For stress and mental stimulation

When your mind is stressed or overstimulated, you will need to clear it before going back to sleep. This is similar to the de-stress technique stated earlier. We have a modified version here which is simpler and quicker. When it's late you just need a quick process to get the immediate concerns off your mind. The mind will keep worrying until it knows the problem is taken care of or you decide it's not important enough to worry about. The trick is to get enough written down so that you know it's taken care of, you won't forget anything and you can come back to it at any time. It's a good idea to keep a pen and pad by the bed, especially if you do a lot of thinking while in bed.

Exercise: Quick mind dump

This exercise is a quick version of the de-stress technique (Chapter 3) to help you get just enough off your mind so that you can sleep.

1 To get started: grab a pen and paper or journal.

2 Divide the pad into two sections and head each section with the following titles 1. Issue on my mind; 2. Insight/solution/schedule.

3 In the first section just write down everything that is keeping you awake. Here are some prompts:

- What's keeping me up?

- What is it that I'm dealing with that I can't solve?

- What am I afraid of?

- What's the most pressing thing I need to do?

- What do I keep forgetting to do?

4 As you are writing you may see solutions to problems, gain some insights or see the need to take some action or schedule an action. Write those down in the insights/solutions/schedule column.

5 *When you've written all you can*, you may find that just getting it all down on paper makes you feel clear enough to go to sleep. If so, great, you can put the pad down and sleep. If this is not the case, then it's time to deal with some of the issues you have written down.

6 For each issue written down with a solution, ask yourself: 'Does that solution satisfy me?' If not, then ask yourself: 'What else is concerning me about this issue?' Write that down.

7 The idea is not to answer every question or deal with every answer. Bring out enough of the issues so you can let them out of your mind and stop worrying sufficiently to fall asleep. If after a while you still have any unresolvable issues just allow yourself to let them go for the night.

8 On completion of the exercise it's time to sleep. Remember not to concern yourself with how many hours you have left to sleep. Just think that you'll have a much better sleep now than you would have had with all the worrying. Any sleep is a blessing.

Issue on my mind	*Insight / solution / schedule*
Worry about redundancy	*Update CV, look for my next move, scale down expenses – still worried though*
Car insurance, service and MOT coming up – how will I find the money?	*Speak to bank about overdraft tomorrow – good for now*
Keep forgetting to check on Mum	*Call tomorrow – schedule a visit – satisfied*
Waiting for buyer to get back but it's been a while	*Speak to buyer tomorrow to get certainty – good for now*

SLEEP RECOVERY

So you wake up tired, haven't had a good night's sleep and you feel pretty lousy. For all our best efforts not every night will be a great night of sleep. What do you do in these situations? A bad night's sleep doesn't have to mean the whole day is ruined. By taking the time to relax upon waking you can undo some of the effects of a poor night's sleep. Simply take the time to do the energy exercises in the morning. Take deep breaths and make sure you relax all the parts of the body where you feel tension or feel tired. Also do not worry about a poor night's sleep. You can always catch up later.

PUSHING THE ENVELOPE: HOW TO THRIVE ON LESS SLEEP

If you are a nine-to-niner or are just temporarily working long hours there will be times when the only way to get things done is to get by on less sleep. This is possible although it may not be medically advisable, but there are times when it happens.

First of all let me outline a common pitfall: when we sleep less, we tend to switch into a survival mode of thinking. We think we are 'surviving' on less sleep. We need to shift this perspective. Whenever we are in survival mode, we tend to be suffering or just getting by. This is mental resistance which will cause more stress.

When sleeping less it is important to minimise this resistance so that we feel less stress. Living on less sleep requires a positive mind-set. Positive emotions such as joy and excitement will carry you through periods of less sleep, so you will need to start finding reasons to be happy.

For example, think back to a time when you experienced a lot of fun in life. Chances are you slept less and were OK with this. Think about children when they are full of excitement; sleeping less doesn't have a major impact on their lives. Just look at any child on the morning of their birthday – you can be pretty sure they were up early, excited by the day ahead, and bounding around full of energy. When they physically need sleep they will crash; when they can't they'll let you know. When they wake up, once again they are excited. Contrast that to when you are in survival mode. When lack of sleep becomes an issue, your life becomes about surviving and not getting enough sleep. Sleep becomes another issue for you to contend with or another stressor. Even when you do catch up on sleep, your experience will be one of temporary relief.

If you are looking to push the envelope and sleep less you probably can go down to five to six hours. You'll need to take more care of yourself, use the energy exercises, ensure that you don't get stressed and supplement it with a very healthy diet (I would consult a nutritionist or health expert on this).

KEY TIPS

- Reduce your sleep time steadily and consistently. Wake up 10 minutes earlier each day until you arrive at an amount of sleep that works for you. Getting up earlier, while hard at first, is the best way to thrive on less. Your body's sleep cycle will adapt and you will feel tired earlier in the day and hence you can go to bed earlier. Doing it the other way, i.e. going to bed earlier, can often be more difficult as you may not be able to get to sleep.

■ If you wake up before your alarm clock goes off and you have had more than five to six hours sleep, just get up. Don't make yourself sleep longer. Create the habit of needing less sleep each day. The body goes through 90-minute sleep cycles, so if you wake up and there is less than 90 minutes before your wakeup time sometimes it's easier just to get up as you may feel groggier if you are interrupted during a sleep cycle.

■ Get your mind on your side. Usually, we have a little voice in our head that evaluates how much sleep we have had and whether we feel our best or not. A common habit people have is to calculate how much sleep they have had and then base on that whether they should or should not feel tired. Stop listening to the little voice in your head when it comes to sleep. Condition your mind to think that anything more than five hours' sleep is good enough.

■ Don't worry about being tired or sleepy. Focusing on tiredness or sleepiness tends to make you feel more tired. Let go of any concerns about it and you'll find that your tiredness or sleepiness will pass.

■ If you feel very sleepy during the day, take a nap. A nap can be as little as five minutes but no more than 30 minutes. Any time over 30 minutes and your body goes into deeper sleep and you'll be groggy upon waking. Grab a nap in the toilet at work if you need to! It's something I used to do.

- Learn to meditate. Meditation can be as restorative as a nap. You can be refreshed in as little as five minutes, although if you are new to meditation it is better to do it for longer: 20–30 minutes is a good time. Good times to meditate are first thing in the morning, during the afternoon or before bed. Meditation before bed really helps you sleep better.

- Get out of bed for no reason. Often, when it is very early, there seems to be no point in getting out of bed. Find something to wake up for and if you can't find it, get up without a reason, just to see what happens. You may surprise yourself.

- Keep your sleeping hours consistent even at the weekends. If you want to sleep longer, limit it to just one hour. I used to sleep in at weekends because I believed it wasn't worth getting out of bed on a Sunday before I had to, but now I get up pretty much the same time (up to an hour later) at weekends as on weekdays.

  Caveat, if you are ill then sleep as long as you need. Give your body enough time to heal itself and fight illness.

GETTING DEEPER: SLEEP PSYCHOLOGY

The following sleep study demonstrates the psychological aspect of sleep. In this sleep study, subjects from similar backgrounds were divided into three groups. They were removed from anything that they could use to check the time or that would give them any indication of how much time had passed, including clocks, light and temperature change.

The first group was told that they would sleep for eight hours. The second group was informed that they would be sleep-deprived and only allowed to sleep for six hours. The third group was told that they would sleep for 10 hours. The group that only slept for six hours complained of sleepiness, irritability and impaired concentration. The group that slept for 10 hours complained of lethargy. The third group reported that they felt fine. In fact, all groups slept the same amount of time – eight hours! They were simply given different information.

How is that for a demonstration of how what we think influences how we feel? People often look at the clock before bed or when waking, to calculate how much sleep they will get or have had. They then use this to determine how tired they should feel.

So I want to introduce a new concept. The tiredness you may feel can be separated from the amount of sleep you've had. Put another way, you can feel tired after having a lot of sleep or feel no tiredness after little sleep. I will demonstrate how to get relief from the feeling of tiredness.

CASE STUDY

I used to think of myself as a morning person. I could never work after 9pm. In fact, my best working hours were between 9am and 1pm. After lunch, my performance went downhill. As soon as 9pm hit, I would become tired and find it hard to concentrate.

It would take me twice as long to complete a project as when I was working at my peak. Once I learnt the secret of tiredness and energy, I noticed that whenever I felt tired, I would experience associated, recurring thoughts of being tired. A mentor once told me that tiredness was psychological, but it took me a few years to listen to this advice and believe it for myself. Once I started letting go of the thoughts of tiredness, I started to feel better, less tired. The tiredness went away, and I started to feel more awake and energised. Now I can easily work until midnight and beyond.

We normally associate tiredness with lack of sleep; which is an obvious cause. However, if we start to think of tiredness as a separate phenomenon from how much sleep we've had, some interesting insights arise. Yes there is the tiredness that comes from lack of sleep but there is also mental fatigue. For example, people with depression often feel tired despite sleeping all day. The mind really has a huge part to play. Mental fatigue comes from how much effort we expect to need to assert now or in the near future or, in other words, our resistance to life. When we are feeling positive about the near future we feel less tired. When we feel negative or uninspired about the future or we resist the future we feel more tired. That is why people who are going through non-clinical depression feel more tired. The future they see makes them feel depressed and as a result they feel tired.

If you are experiencing tiredness while getting enough sleep, or if you feel tired all the time, the first question to ask is:

What does your future look like? Are you looking forward to it, dreading it, resisting it, or do you see it as 'just another day'?

If you aren't looking forward to your future, chances are that your outlook on life or resistance to it is contributing to your tiredness. If you believe your tiredness or fatigue is medical or nutritional, please see a doctor or examine your diet more carefully.

Let's take a deeper look at tiredness. To find the cause of tiredness, we must examine the sensations or feelings associated with it. Tiredness has physical and psychological components.

For me, physical tiredness occurs as a kind of cloudiness in my brain, which makes it harder to think. There is tension in my eyes, yet they feel heavy; I also feel tension in my forehead and around my neck and shoulders. I feel unable to concentrate. These sensations are associated with the thought that I am tired. This is the psychological component. There is a link between the physical and psychological components. Notice when you're tired what tiredness actually feels like. What sensations do you experience?

Now try and let go of the idea 'I'm tired' or replace it with 'I feel wide awake or energetic'. When you give up the thought or replace it, you'll find sensations go away. The psychological component affects the physical one. In fact, when you concentrate on being wide awake (or energetic or inspired) and you let that become a sensation in your body, the tiredness will disappear! The trick is to maintain the wide-awake thought. Replace the tiredness idea that is usually a default. You need to think it and have an expectation that this is true. You are self-reporting and then waiting for that report to be true.

To make this easier to understand let's look at the thoughts. When you feel tired you have a thought which says 'I'm tired', you also have the sensation of tiredness in your body. Now consider that tiredness is just an experience in the body. This experience is triggered by your mind; in other words, tiredness is a recurring idea that you tell yourself. The thought that you are tired triggers the sensations of tiredness. Your mind then 'believes' that it is indeed feeling tired, and yet another thought loop is created. In this case, we can create a tired state of mind.

The thought associated with tiredness is a deep thought – it is part conscious and part subconscious, a communication from mind to body. To relieve tiredness requires a certain 'unravelling' of this thought process. By giving up the thoughts and sensations of tiredness, and replacing them with energetic ones, you will feel more awake.

Exercise

1 When you are tired, notice the experience of being tired. What are the sensations in your eyes, head and body? If you are not tired right now, repeat to yourself, 'I feel so tired'. Do you see how you can make yourself tired just by suggesting it?

▶

2 Now, remember a time when you were excited and alert. What are the sensations in your eyes, brain, head and body? Practise telling yourself, 'I am so wide awake and happy!' Notice the sensations in your eyes, head and body.

3 Practise alternating between being tired and awake just by thinking of it.

Once you have mastered this, you will be able to eliminate tiredness and extend the amount of time you can be effective way into the night or early morning. This technique will get you anywhere from 30 minutes to a few hours of extra awake time. At some point it will be more difficult to do, as you become exhausted, but it is a good exercise to extend wakefulness when you need it. I use it when working late at night on a deadline.

Also practise this technique if you feel tired when waking up in the morning. This will help you feel wide awake. When most people are tired, they try to fight the tiredness by pushing through. This creates more stress and uses more energy. By using these techniques and just letting go of the thoughts and feelings of tiredness, you let your soft energy come into effect. After some practice, you will be able to rejuvenate your eyes and any other tension hotspots by directing soft energy there.

Summary

There is a lot of contradictory research on sleep. We can conclude that getting six to eight hours is fine. Focus on the quality of sleep. Going to bed relaxed with nothing on your mind will help you get more effective sleep. Following a good sleep routine will get you in the habit of sleeping well.

Our sleep psychology, how we think about sleep, has a big impact on the quality of sleep we have and how tired we feel. Eliminate worry about sleep. This will help you to go to bed more easily, to sleep more soundly and recover more easily if you have a bad night's sleep.

For additional information and resources on sleep go to: www.energyequationbook.com/resources

CHAPTER 5

Releasing the brakes – using the power of thought

IN THE ZONE

We've covered increasing personal energy and sleeping better. Now let's look at how we can become more effective in life: both at work, in terms of focus and concentration, and in other areas of our life. Let's look at living in the zone. The zone is when we are fully alert and operating at our best.

It occurs when what we've been working on becomes the only thing we experience. We are completely immersed in what we are doing, and the concept of time disappears. We become focused, more productive and experience a sense of accomplishment for the time spent.

The zone is a place of pure focus. It's somewhere athletes strive to be so that their mind and body work in perfect sync and their movements seem to flow without conscious effort. They can use all of their training and do their best without any distracting thoughts.

Although as intellectual workers we don't use our bodies as much, the brain is the 'muscle' of choice for us instead of the legs or arms, this ability to achieve pure focus is still achievable and very desirable.

Through mental training and exercise we can get into a resourceful state of mind that enables us to make the best use of our brains. From there we can become more productive; we are able to learn more quickly and better absorb information and express creativity. The brain becomes like a sponge, and resistance disappears as we do repetitive tasks more easily and the mental or emotional resistance diminishes as we release the brakes.

If you could get into this mental state more often, you would be more relaxed, focused and productive. Even if you didn't get everything done, you would feel you did good work and operated at 100% capacity. You would learn more and progress faster.

Many of us are clamouring for this experience; with all the busyness and interruption of daily life we want periods of calm and focus when we can just get things done. We do experience this from time to time but we would all like to reach this state more often. With so many things on our minds, it can sometimes seem that getting into the zone is a matter of luck. Things that usually get in the way of reaching this state are constant interruptions, worries about the future, procrastination and concerns about all the things that need to be done.

So how do you get into this state? Let's look at how the athlete might do it. Here is the champion diver about to do a complicated dive; he may be preoccupied with the crowd, worrying about whether he will do his manoeuvre correctly, or fearful that he hasn't trained enough. But just as he is about to get started, he quietens the mind, focuses on what he needs to do, and then begins to leap from the diving board into the air. Just when he decides and takes off, he enters the zone, and the sound of the crowd disappears. He executes his moves flawlessly, as he has trained to do for some time.

We also experience this when we can get away from all distractions; when we can quieten the mind and find a place where we can do what we need to do. But usually we don't get there as consistently as we would like. It doesn't just stop at our work life. You can apply getting into the zone at any time. It's being in the present moment. It's like going on a romantic date and feeling the whole world disappear; it's spending time with your kids and just having a great time. It's having fun with good friends and time just standing still. When you are enjoying yourself and time seems to fly by or just stand still then you know you are in the zone. This book is about having a life in the zone. This is the kind of life where you can live with joy, productivity and fulfilment, while equally enjoying both work and play. Getting into the zone is all about learning to shut out the distractions, quieten the mind and focus our thoughts. So let's learn how to do this.

So far, we have learned how to use our mind to increase our energy and to relieve stress and tiredness. We've learned a little about how the mind works and its effect on the body when we get stressed. These techniques have been using the mind to effect a change in our experience. We are now going to explore the mind in more depth.

Your mind is highly powerful and, with the right training, you can direct it to improve your wellbeing and eliminate stress in your life. One powerful observation of this phenomenon is the placebo effect. This has been demonstrated in many medical studies. A patient who expects a drug, for example a pain killer, is given a tablet that actually does nothing. The patient's expectation of getting better makes them get better. Numerous scientific studies have confirmed that placebos work. What is more interesting is that if our thoughts can have such a physical impact on our bodies then it may be a simple matter to use our thoughts to get rid of stress, to get more energy and to feel better emotionally.

For example, if a placebo can get rid of a pounding headache then maybe you can bypass the placebo and train your brain to get rid of the headache by itself. Imagine being able to quickly get rid of the pain of an impending headache without tablets

Let's begin by looking at how the mind works.

THINKING, CHEMISTRY AND EMOTIONS

The brain is a complex system of more than 100 billion neurons, which communicate with each other and with the body through electrical impulses and biochemical messengers that constantly flow throughout the body.

Our every thought produces a biochemical reaction in the brain. The brain then releases chemicals that transmit to the body, acting as the messengers of our thoughts. These chemicals produce associated feelings in the body. In effect, every thought you have produces a chemical that matches a feeling in your body. For example, if you think hard enough and really imagine that you are swimming in shark-infested waters and are sure a shark is coming towards you, your heart will start to race, your palms will begin to sweat, and you will feel fear. Conversely, when you think happy or positive thoughts, for example thoughts of you lying on the beach on holiday, the brain produces chemicals that make you feel happy. Thoughts produce feelings.

When the body responds to a thought by having a feeling, the brain responds to the way the body is feeling and generates thoughts that produce corresponding chemical messengers. Your thoughts begin to validate your feelings. Thinking creates feeling, which creates thinking – in a continuous loop. This happens all of the time. Sometimes it is the thought that drives the feeling, sometimes a feeling comes up from your subconsciousness which influences your thoughts. Generally when things come up in life we have an emotional reaction or a thought which in turn influences our actions.

For example, if you are driving along having a great day and then someone cuts in front of you, your reaction will go from pleasant to angry in an instant. If you continue to ruminate on how someone cut you up, you may get increasingly angry which then triggers more angry thoughts. You may notice other things that make you angry or you become alert to things annoying you. Your thoughts influenced your emotions and then your emotions influenced your thinking.

In addition, your perception of the world was influenced by your emotional state and your thinking. Actually your perception of the world influenced the first thought when the driver cut in on you. These perceptions of the world were influenced by past experiences and conclusions about the world, which are earlier thinking patterns. So our thinking influences our emotions, which influence our perception of reality, which also influence our reactions. These are all intertwined, but if we start with our own thoughts we can begin to control our emotions and our perception of reality.

Thoughts are the key determinants of reality

Good news! If you can control your thoughts, you can control how you feel emotionally and physically. Therefore you need to work on having thoughts that are more empowering. Just as you can become stressed, you can also clear your mind, calm your body and even control the muscles that cause tension and headaches. The mind is the key.

THE POWER OF THOUGHT

So how can you use your thoughts to your advantage to take control of your feelings, body and sleep patterns? You are already doing this to some extent. Can you relate to any of these examples?

- You tell yourself that you are not good at maths, so when you come to a maths problem in life, you instantly remind yourself that you are bad at maths and hesitate to answer rather than just getting on and doing the sums.

- You look at the clock at night, calculate how much sleep you are going to get and determine how tired you will feel tomorrow. Consequently when you get up the next day you are tired.

- You look at the clock in the morning, calculate how much sleep you have had and decide how tired you are.

- You wake up feeling tired, you get annoyed that you are tired or down. You then trigger the emotions of feeling down, which only add to the feeling of being tired, thus making you feel even more tired and miserable.

- On Sunday, you feel down about the fact that it is work tomorrow. You are miserable the next day – Monday – as you have already decided that Mondays are depressing.

- When you are confident about speaking in public, what do you tell yourself? Contrast that to when you do not feel confident.

- You complain to yourself in the morning about how tired you are and how much work you have to do. Your morning turns out to be a struggle and funnily enough you feel tired.

- Whenever you try something new your default reaction is 'I can't do this' or 'I don't know how to do that'.

Do you get the picture? All these thoughts are examples of how we create our experiences of life with our thoughts on an everyday basis. With these thoughts going on, we are already creating our feelings and experiences. So we can consciously train our minds to create energising, empowering experiences.

I like looking at the field of sports for how our thoughts influence our learning. I attended adult gymnastics for a period and it was amazing to see the learning speeds. There were gymnasts who had been training for a while and reached a plateau while new, inexperienced people would come in and accelerate quite quickly.

I noticed that those who reached their plateau didn't believe that they could improve any further. I remember one girl in particular, whenever she was pushed to do something new, would instantly say 'I can't do it'. Even when she tried to do a new move she did it half-heartedly and expected to fail. She had been at the same ability level for years just maintaining what she could do. I noticed the contrast with newbie gymnasts who just wanted to learn. They weren't concerned with whether they could or could not do something; they just wanted to learn. Many of them surpassed the experienced girl. Successful people always start with a belief that they can do something; they have an intention to learn and improve.

These examples just hint at the mind's capabilities. We could have more of these experiences if we let the mind do its job. So we know we are using our thoughts all the time. Let's look at what happens when we direct our thoughts and use intentions.

THE POWER OF INTENTION

An intention is a focused thought of what you intend to do. It is a simple principle, but a powerful one. When we are being determined we are using intention. Intention creates clarity. For example, have you noticed that when you decide to buy a certain car, you seem to notice all the cars of the same make and model everywhere you go? This is called the Reticular Activating System (RAS), which is a function of intention. Because we have an intention, our brains start to tune into information that we would otherwise bypass.

INTENTIONS THAT WORK

Stating an intention clearly helps make it more powerful. Here are some examples.

My intention is:

■ To delegate this task to Dave so that he is absolutely clear on what I want and is empowered to carry out that task.

■ To complete two sections of the market report in the next hour.

■ To leave this meeting with clear ideas of what is next and having felt like something was accomplished.

■ To have a good time with my friends and let them know that even though I am busy, I am there for them.

When our minds are super-focused, we can turn all of our attention to a thought, action or object. The frontal lobe in our brains will filter out all the random sensory stimuli in the environment. When this occurs, we are in the best mental position to intentionally learn, create and perform a skill.

Most people do not use intentions or are unintentional in their activities. They go about life without a clear intention of what they want to achieve. This is normal as it is not something you learn at school.

For example, consider how often you have attended meetings in which, although there is an agenda, half the people in attendance are there because they feel they have to be there, and consequently are not focused on having a productive meeting. Those meetings seem to go around in circles. Now contrast that to meetings where the attendees are highly intentional, contributing to the discussion, paying attention and focusing on the issues.

USING THE POWER OF INTENTION

Using intention is simple; it just takes remembering to do it. Creating an intention starts with stating to yourself what you will do. Here are some examples:

- If you are finishing a report, state in your mind that you are going to create a great report that people will love.
- If you are cold-calling a client, you have an intention to create a sale.
- If you are spending time with family, you may have an intention to have a great time and show your family how much you love them.

When you experience frustration or feel like procrastinating, return to your intention. For example, while writing this text I can easily find other distractions. I am tempted to go off on a tangent into the science of almost everything, research it, go on the web and then find myself side-tracked by other subjects – all of which I enjoy, but then I find myself going off-track, so I have to bring myself back to what I intend to communicate.

THE POWER OF INTENTION IN COMMUNICATION

Having an intention is one of the most powerful things to bring to communication. Having an intention in an email keeps your email succinct and communicates exactly what the other person needs to hear. If you have an argument with someone with an intention to resolve the situation (rather than to prove your point) you will be more effective in your communication.

A good question to ask oneself in communication is, 'What do I want the other person to know? What do I want to communicate?'

Does your intention move the action forward or backward?

HIDDEN AGENDAS/INTENTIONS

Often when we don't set an intention, we have a hidden intention, hidden agenda or ulterior motive that counteracts what we are really doing. This hidden intention may even be hidden from your own view. Your actions say one thing but the effect is something different. You may have seen this in meetings where people are speaking, but something seems off. They are saying one thing which makes sense intellectually but what they are saying does not square with the message you receive. For example, in a project meeting, someone comes up with a suggestion that seems irrelevant. It looks as though they are contributing but actually they just want to look as if they are contributing and making an effort.

Here are some examples of hidden intentions I've noticed in many a meeting:

- To prove how clever I am.
- To prove that I am always right.
- To prove that it is their fault.
- To disrupt this project so that I can get out of it.
- To let people know how busy I am so that they will stop giving me more work.
- To assert authority and control a situation.

Hidden agendas are a normal human habit and there is nothing inherently wrong with this. However, it helps to be mindful of your own hidden agendas so that you don't sabotage your or someone else's efforts.

WHEN INTENTION GETS SPOOKY

Intention helps keep you focused. There are some advanced ways in which we can train our minds. Have you ever said you are going to wake up at certain time and woken up just before your alarm clock sounded? You created an intention in your mind and trusted that your body would act on it, and it did. You in effect programmed your subconscious mind and it went to work

A ZEN MIND – THE POWER OF CONCENTRATION

Have you noticed how easy it is to get distracted and go off-track even when you start with good intentions? In this age of information, it is quite easy to get distracted when bombarded with emails, messages, blogs, articles and social media updates. While in the past concentration was valued, now it seems even more important than ever.

I have to be disciplined when I am on the internet because I will often drift off to a great piece of news, article or posting that catches my eye. There is so much interesting information out there but that doesn't necessarily make it useful. So how do you keep focused with all this distraction? The best way is to keep a clear mind. Have you noticed how much we clutter our brain with needless information and things to remember? When you were younger and had less on your plate, do you recall how much easier it was to remember things?

The more you clutter your brain the less you allow it to do its full work. The brain's best application is original, intellectual processing, creativity and thought. However, most of us are running too many thought processes in the background and are slowing down our brain computer. These processes are the endless thought loops of the things you have to do, the things you are trying to remember, the things you are worried about, and the things about which you daydream.

The more thoughts you get out of the way the more you can focus. In addition, when you unclutter your mind, you allow your intuition and creativity to work. Ideally we want to put all the thoughts, ideas and the things to do in a system that allows us to deal with them when the time is right. (We will explore this in Chapter 9.)

Meditation helps concentration

Not only a great way to get rid of stress, meditation enables you to keep your mind clear and improves your power of focus and concentration. The main advantage of meditation is allowing your thoughts to be there without always needing to act upon them. Research has shown that meditation increases the ability to concentrate, have more control over emotions and reduce stress by creating more neural connections in the frontal lobes of the brain (the seat of higher brain functions). Meditation is a great antidote to the information overload and level of distraction we experience with the use of the internet, email and social media. There are a variety of ways to meditate. These range from focusing on breathing to using guided meditation.

Simple meditation

One of the simplest ways to meditate is to focus on your breathing. Follow your breath as you breathe in and out. Allow your thoughts to come and go; notice yourself noticing your thoughts. A common thing that stops people meditating is becoming frustrated when their minds drift off. More than likely your mind will drift off, even if you've been meditating for a long time. Don't worry, just notice it and come back to the meditation. Be an observer of your thoughts rather than getting caught up in them. You will benefit even if your mind wanders off. It is a training ground for developing more focus and concentration, so build up slowly. Think of it as gym for the mind. (For more information on meditation and resources go to **www.energyequationbook.com/resources**)

OVERCOMING THE MONKEY MIND

CASE STUDY

Sally gets up on a Monday morning feeling tired, as usual, and she engages in the same old routine – the Monday morning mental complaining. She starts by noticing how tired she is; then the mind chatter begins – that internal dialogue that Sally has with herself. It usually goes something like this:

'Ugh, the alarm, what time is it?'

'It's 6.30am.'

'It can't be; I just went to bed. Have I even slept?'

'I should get up.'

'I'll just snooze for five more minutes.'

▶

'Ok.'

'How do I feel, anyway?'

'I feel exhausted. What did I do over the weekend?'

'Nothing major. I shouldn't feel this bad.'

'I should have gone to bed on time instead of watching that film last night.'

'Am I coming down with something? Maybe I should call in sick.'

'I do feel a bit weak. Do I have a temperature? I feel a bit hot.'

'But I need to go in to work; I have to do that project.'

'Oh, yeah.'

'I'd better get up, then.'

Several minutes after pressing the snooze alarm, Sally finally drags herself out of bed. Whilst in the shower, her mental chatter continues. Sally still cannot shake the tiredness...

'Why am I so tired? How much sleep did I get?'

'About seven hours.'

'Well, I shouldn't feel this tired.'

'Yeah, and I didn't drink this weekend. I only had one glass of red wine.'

'It's so strange ... I wish I could shake this feeling. I can't really afford to be tired today. I have a lot to do, and I really need to be alert.'

'What time will I finish work tonight? I should really get an early night so I can recover.'

'Oh, damn, I'll probably finish late tonight, and then I have to meet Jane for dinner after work. I promised her, and I've cancelled twice already, so I should meet her.'

'I probably won't get home until 10.30 or 11. By the time I get to bed, it will be around 12, so I will have no time to catch up on sleep tonight. I hope she can't make it and cancels.'

'OK, so tonight is out for an early night. When is the next time I can have an early night and sleep in?'

'Well, there is gym Tuesday, and the project deadline is Wednesday, which means late nights until then. So it looks like the next time I'll get an early night will probably be Thursday if work goes OK and then on Saturday we're meeting Dave's parents. So the next lie-in is on Sunday. Gosh I'm going to be exhausted by the weekend. I hope I can make it through the week and still perform on this project.'

With no time for breakfast Sally rushes to catch the train to work on time. Like a lot of Mondays the journey is a nightmare, Sally doesn't get a seat on the train and spends the journey under someone's sweaty armpit. The train is 10 minutes late and the journey would be even worse if Sally were awake enough to notice it. Sally remains in a half-stressed, half-asleep state.

After grabbing coffee and a croissant on the way in, Sally arrives at work feeling a bit stressed. Luckily, the morning begins slowly, as is usual for Mondays. Most people are just gearing themselves up for the week

▶

ahead. Sally plods through the report she is working on, hoping she has enough resources about her to make it through the day.

After two glorious uninterrupted hours in the morning, her boss comes through with the first disruption to the day: he asks her to work on the urgent last-minute changes on the project, which was supposed to have been sent out last Friday.

'I worked hard last week to get this done. Why didn't he give me this feedback on Friday?' Sally thinks to herself.

By the time she finishes the last-minute changes, two hours have been taken out of the day. Now she has less time to do the items on her to-do list.

The rest of the day continues, with small, five-minute interruptions here and there, and by mid-afternoon Sally's day has been thrown out of whack. She's completed the main items on her list, but she finishes the day behind in her schedule with more items on her to-do list than she started with.

By 8pm, Sally calls it a day; she's not going to get it all done today. She'll just go in early tomorrow. 'Damn, this is already an awful week.'

Sally ends the day exhausted and frustrated, feeling like she's been battling an invisible force called time.

Is Sally's experience similar to yours? It's Monday, and Sally has already concluded that she is going to have a long and tiring week. She has created a day, a week even, of problems and exhaustion, and the best thing she can look forward to is an early night on Thursday and then making it to the weekend. Her week has become about surviving until the weekend. Many people go through the same experience every day. How many of us doom ourselves to days or weeks of struggle, annoyance and effort by listening to our mental chatter?

Can you see how we create our day by constantly telling ourselves how tired we are, or how terrible the day or week is going to be? Sally's tiredness could have passed after

10 minutes in the morning by doing the right exercises as mentioned, but by constantly focusing on how tired she was, Sally remained tired and stressed the whole day.

We constantly have thoughts like these going on. We have a million thoughts per day going through our heads. Our reptilian brain is always alert for ways to protect us, which is why our brains act like this.

HOW TO COMBAT MIND CHATTER

We all have mind chatter, the little voice in our head that provides a running commentary on our life, how we are feeling, what is happening in our world, what others are doing, and so on. To deal with mind chatter, it's best to start as early as possible in the morning as this is when you have your 'me' time to really be able to talk to yourself. If you've got a busy day sometimes you don't have time to consider what thoughts are going on in your head and you're more likely to think on autopilot. Also a negative mind in the morning can influence your whole day. Here is the four-step process you can use.

Stage 1 – It is time to deal with the mind chatter

Usually, we pay too much attention to our thoughts. Consider your brain as a computer that picks up thoughts from your subconscious mind and generates new ones based on your subconscious programming. This programming has come from your past, stored memories from your upbringing, from your parents, from society, from what you read in the news, from your peers and colleagues. We do have new creative thoughts as well but the majority of our thinking is based on our past experiences from our reptilian brain. It's rather like having a worrying mother in your head.

You don't have to respond to every thought you get. If your parent has ever reprimanded you for taking bad advice from someone, you may be familiar with the saying, 'If someone told you to put your head down a toilet, would you do it?' Treat your mental chatter like this. We all have positive and negative thoughts; and creative or destructive ones. We don't have to obey or even pay attention to all our thoughts.

So to deal with the mind chatter, let it run in the background and just observe your thoughts without reacting to them. When my mind chatter runs out of line, I just think or say to myself, 'Blah, blah, blah…' This negates your thoughts – it tells your brain not to take them seriously. Keep doing this until you get tired of listening to the same record, and then let the thoughts quieten down.

Stage 2 – Acknowledge your feelings, but don't get stuck with them

The first stage deals with not taking mind chatter too seriously. However, along with these thoughts come feelings. The feelings tend to generate thoughts analysing why you are feeling that way. When people have negative emotions they tend to want to change or suppress them. So first acknowledge how your body feels; allow your feelings to be there, and let them go when you are ready.

Feelings change during the day. Sometimes you wake up feeling lousy but feel fine, or even great, just a few hours later. So if you feel lousy in the morning, just say to yourself: 'Right now I feel lousy, but it will pass, and soon I will feel better.' Then let it go – do not listen to any other thoughts about how you feel.

Stage 3 – Take creative control over your thoughts and feelings

As we have seen with the tiredness exercise, we can make ourselves feel better with our thoughts.

Tell yourself you feel great, think of something beautiful or inspiring, or remember a time when you felt happy. Notice your feelings as they begin to change. Feel the sensation of happiness. If you have difficulty with this, fake it until you make it. Change your physiology – stand up straight and walk tall. When we change our physiology, we start to feel better. A good time to do this is in the morning. You don't have to have happy thoughts every day. Sometimes you need to get on with your day and go through what you are feeling. However, the happier you are the better you will feel.

Stage 4 – Utilise motivating reasons

When we have something great to wake up for in the morning, we tend to be motivated and begin the day well, we have a more positive mind chatter. Find something to get up for in the morning. Think of one thing about your job that excites you. What else could you add to your day to be even more excited about? Make getting up early a victory, even if it's just an extra 10 minutes to put on the laundry before leaving the house. Another useful thing to do is to have a visual reminder of a goal, perhaps an inspiring quote, or a picture that motivates you on a wall or door where you will see it regularly. I put notices on my front door so I will see them when I leave the house.

Summary

Our thoughts are powerful; our thinking influences our emotions which influence our actions and our perceptions of the world. These are all intertwined to some extent but it is over our thoughts that we can exercise some influence.

An intention is a focused thought of what we intend to do. By focusing our thoughts in this way, we can become more focused on what we want to accomplish and cut out the background thoughts and feelings that influence our life.

CHAPTER 6

Ten steps to creating a great day

We've now covered almost everything you need to create an energised life, to live life in the zone and have more time for yourself. Let's look at how you can put it into practice. You've learned how to energise your body, how to get rid of stress, how to use your mind to focus and concentrate better and how to get more effective sleep. So how do you use it?

Knowledge without the practice won't make a difference to you. Ideally you'll want to habitualise the contents of the book so that it becomes second nature for you. I've created a 10-point daily action plan to help you do this. You don't need to use all of the steps all the time but doing so will make the biggest difference.

THE 10 STEPS FOR LIVING LIFE IN THE ZONE

How to get into the zone:

1 Begin the morning by clearing away any mental chatter, energising your body; then create how you want the day to go.

2 Once you get to work, start the workday with a bang by focusing on what you would like to achieve by the end of the day.

3 Use intentions: create an intention for each piece of work that you do. Work in concentration 'bursts' to help you.

4 Maintain momentum by minimising distractions and managing energy.

5 Take your breaks, especially lunch.

6 Remember to perk up your energy when you need to.

7 Keep the last hour of your day to focus on completing work and leaving.

8 De-stress, acknowledge what you accomplished and clear your mind at the end of the day.

9 Enjoy yourself the rest of the evening; have fun.

10 Sleep or rest well.

1 CLEAR OUT ANY MENTAL CHATTER AND ENERGISE

The morning is the most important part of the day. This is when you need to set yourself up nicely for the day ahead. In the story in the previous chapter we saw from Sally how **not** to create the day. Do you ever start the morning off badly and the rest of the day seems to go downhill from there? It's as if you got out of the wrong side of the bed. Let's say you wake up feeling tired or exhausted, then your train is delayed or you get stuck in traffic – the day starts with some small incident that annoys you, and then a few more incidents occur, and the accumulation of annoying incidents results in you having a bad day.

You must also have had the opposite experience, in which you started the morning off well and everything seemed to go smoothly from there. People are exceptionally nice to you, work goes without a hitch, you find a parking spot easily, your train comes exactly on time, other 'lucky' things happen all day, the universe is out to make sure you have a great day.

If you haven't given much thought to your mornings, now is the time to start. You can choose how you want your day to go every morning, but first start by eliminating any mind chatter (as we saw in the Chapter 5). This will clear any mental negativity out of your system. This is the easiest thing to do when you've just woken up, and you're still half asleep.

Remember, if you wake up feeling tired it's not the end of the world – your body can recover. We have all had the experience of starting off the day feeling tired and feeling great by the end of it.

Next use an energiser exercise (see Chapter 2) to clear away the effects of a poor night's sleep or any residual tiredness.

This should take approximately 15 minutes. If you are rushed for time, sit down and do a few minutes of deep breathing (this can also be done on a train).

2 BEGIN THE DAY WELL

Now you have muted mind chatter, let's look at how to create your day, increasing your chances of having a great one. This is really making up an intention of how you want the day to go. The most important thing is to believe that you can create a great day with your mental attitude. Sometimes even your best intentions will not result in a perfect day (problems and challenges do crop up), but when you set out to have a good day you will see your problems and challenges in a different light and be better equipped to deal with them. There are two components to creating your day:

1 The goal for today, what you want to accomplish.

2 The context or theme, how you choose to view or perceive the day.

By changing your perspective and expectations for the day you can change how the day is for you, put yourself in a positive frame of mind, and allow yourself to see problems as challenges or minor obstacles. Normally when we are overworked or stressed we tend to have a negative or survival view of life which helps keep us stressed and exhausted. By actively creating a context or theme we can shift this point of view, provide more motivation and give ourselves more energy.

Take time to get some mental quiet and create your day. Take the time to do this even if you have to do it on the train to work, or in the parking lot in your car for five minutes.

Creating goals

Create a goal that's achievable during the day. It doesn't need to be work related or big, just motivating. If it is big then chunk it down to make it achievable. Sometimes you don't want to create a goal and that's fine: you can create a theme for the day and see what happens. This can bring pleasant surprises.

Themes – creating the context for the day

A theme allows you to create an experience for the day. Creating a theme brings focus and a sense of creating something new and unexpected. A theme can be an attitude that you intend to take on, such as being peaceful, or can also be an assertion or hypothesis of how the day will go. For example, you can assert, 'There are opportunities everywhere today, and I am out to grab them.'

You can use an analogy regarding how you will respond to the events of the day. For example, I often use martial arts as an analogy for my life, and I like to think of myself as being a nimble martial artist, responding to any events in the day with calm and decisive action while using minimal force for maximum effect. Choose something that motivates or inspires you.

A theme isn't the truth; it's just a new perspective that you can take on for the day. You can create themes any way you like. Creating a theme gets you out of the rut of doing the same thing day in, day out. Change your theme often. Below you will find some themes I made up. If you create the theme of Fun, you make your day fun, you look for the fun things in life and for opportunities for fun or you allow others to have fun around you. Imagine if you chose the theme 'Today is the first day of the rest of my life'. How would the world appear?

Themes

General themes of the day

- Fun
- Velocity – things are done with speed and ease
- Attention to detail
- Clarity
- Gratitude for my life
- Peace
- Wax on, wax off – everything I am doing is preparing me for something greater
- There is an abundance of opportunity
- Love is everywhere

How I will be today

- Today I will see the good in others
- Today is the first day of the rest of my life
- I am the star in my show
- I have the Midas touch
- All obstacles are lessons in life
- I will experience all the miracles of life
- I look for the wisdom in everything
- I am gorgeous
- Life and people are supporting me
- I am an oasis of calm in the midst of chaos

Metaphors for life

- All the world is a stage and we are merely players
- Playing the game

- Bending with the wind, surrendering to life – bowing, but not breaking

Derailments

Even though you've created your day you may get derailed. You will often encounter obstacles and events that can disrupt your intentions for a great day. Do not allow yourself to be derailed by incidents that dent your sense of calm or purpose. Common derailments in the morning are commuting incidents, being squashed on a packed train, encountering an emergency at work, or a huge inbox of emails.

Deal with these derailments by allowing them to be there; this is non-resistance. Accept that these events happen, but don't react. Allow your mind to be peaceful and non-reactive. Look at waiting time and travel delays as extra time to practise body awareness and harnessing energy.

Start work with a bang

You've created your day, so now it's time to work. Decide exactly when you will start the main bulk of the work. This could be the first thing you do, or just after you check your email. I recommend spending no more than 15 minutes checking emails and responding to quick enquiries. Check to see if anything interferes with what you have already planned.

Dedicate at least one hour (preferably two) to doing the main bulk of your work, otherwise known as 'eating the frog'. The frog is the work that will really move you forward. If you did nothing else in the day then it would be the work you would be satisfied with having completed. Do all your other work after you have 'eaten the frog'. If you had to do any urgent activities in the morning, do that next. If you are an evening person, you may feel more productive in the afternoon. Do an alternative activity that is important but that doesn't require you to be at the peak of your productivity.

By the way, it is possible to become a morning person or an 'anytime' person. It's all a matter of your belief and the way you harness your energy. I used to be a morning person and my day was pretty much ruined if I didn't complete the bulk of my work by midday. Now I've trained myself to be productive in the morning, afternoon and evening.

3 USE INTENTIONS AND WORK IN CONCENTRATION BURSTS

Before each task, **state your intention**. Stating your intention galvanises your mind for the things you want to achieve and helps you avoid procrastination. You can even write it down and refer to it or have it in a calendar to remind you.

Determine your concentration limit. This is the amount of time you can focus on doing one thing and continue to be productive. It can be anywhere from 30 minutes to two hours; for most people, it will be one to two hours. Studies have shown that the optimal time is 90 minutes, in line with our natural circadian cycles. At the end of your concentration period take a break of 10–15 minutes. Include some stretching to release tension and improve circulation. When you come back, remind yourself of your intention and restart your work.

4 KEEPING MOMENTUM

Here are some tips for keeping your momentum going when you are in the flow:

Manage your interruptions

Interruptions are one of the most annoying barriers to productivity. They are a part of life and a necessary evil at work. It has been proven that each time you are interrupted it takes 5–6 minutes to settle back into what you were doing and get back to the same momentum. If you work in a high interruption environment, then this can easily add an extra hour or two to your day, especially when you add the actual time of the interruption. The more we control our interruptions, the better. I suggest creating some designated time when everyone in the office knows you cannot be interrupted, even if you set aside only 30 minutes. The best way to create a no-interruption zone is to close your email and internet browser. Turn off or divert your phone. Put a sign on your door or cubicle, put on headphones, or go to a meeting room. You may need to convince your manager of the importance of your interruption-free time.

Dealing with interruptions

There are times when we just can't help the interruptions, so we need to deal with whatever comes up. The trick is to be able to switch between mental tasks quickly. You can facilitate this by calmly dealing with the interruption rather than getting annoyed. Getting upset triggers additional thoughts which can make the distraction worse.

A great way to pick up momentum after an interruption is to mark where you are in your work at the time of being interrupted. Either type it into your program if you are using a word editor or a spreadsheet, highlighting the text you are working on, or make a note. Write down what you have just done and what you were going to do next, along with any critical thoughts you need to remember.

Minimise your own interruptions or your 'ADHD'

Slightly less annoying than external interruptions are those from your own mind. When you have a lot on your mind, it will interrupt you with things to do, things you forgot to do and things you really should do. If your mind won't rest until it knows those to-dos are taken care of, just keep a pad nearby and write down any of your thoughts of things to do. You will review the pad at a more convenient time. If there is anything critical then obviously do it. But we want to spend most of our time doing important and meaningful work rather than flitting from one thing to another, accomplishing little.

Another great tip to keep you focused is to use a productivity timer. Get a countdown timer – you can use one on your phone, computer or a kitchen timer. Set the timer to go off every 5–10 minutes. This will bring back your attention to what you are doing. If you're doing lots of mini tasks then aim to complete a task by the time the timer goes off.

For example, completing an email every five minutes. If you are working on a larger project just use it as a pacer to keep you focused on what you are doing and prevent you from going off-track.

Maintaining energy

The best way to maintain your energy levels is to enjoy yourself, have as much fun and excitement as possible and not get stressed. If you are having a stressful day, deal with the stress immediately. Use energising exercises (see Chapter 2). Just two minutes of proper breathing can make all the difference.

5 BREAK UP YOUR DAY – TAKE YOUR LUNCH

By working in concentration bursts you split up your day. Taking breaks to go outside and get air or walk around is highly recommended, especially if you are stationary at your desk most of the day. It will help your back, prevent any repetitive strain injuries and help your eyes. The most important thing here is to take your lunch break. Many people use the lunch break as a time-saving exercise, just grabbing some food quickly. Don't. Take your time. Do not work during lunch. If you want to have energy throughout the day, you need to use your lunch break properly. Remind yourself that lunch is for recovery and revitalisation.

Don't fall into the false economy of time-saving illusion either. Skipping 30 minutes of lunch may mean you leave work

30 minutes earlier but it will also mean your energy is far more likely to be depleted at the end of the day. So those 30 minutes of time will cost you more than 30 minutes in useful time when you have the energy to do something.

Have an enjoyable lunch break, after which you will return relaxed and rejuvenated. Remember, a relaxing lunch break will help you properly and efficiently digest your food. Eat foods that you can digest efficiently.

6 REMEMBER YOUR ENERGY

Generally, energy levels go down after lunch as the body digests the food. Use this time for work that doesn't require as much mental effort, such as work that involves active collaboration, phone calls, etc.

If you need an energy pick-me-up, use energiser exercises (Chapter 2) or try having a catnap.

7 THE HOME RUN

A common trap is taking on work at the end of the day. Anything taken on an hour before you need to leave is likely to have you working later than anticipated. Set a boundary here. Reserve an hour before the end of your workday to complete what you are working on and then schedule activities for the next day. I call this the home run. You are completing things for the day. Don't allow any work to interrupt the home run. Don't take on any new work; just complete what there is for the day. If you need to, go into a meeting room or tell everyone you are working on a deadline and can't take anything else on for today.

8 END OF THE WORKDAY – DE-STRESS

Take the time to let go of the workday. Take at least 10 minutes to review the day. What did you accomplish, what is left over, what needs to be scheduled for the next day? This is a great way to finish the day and let go. You want to feel clear about what you accomplished, what is still left over and what will be done the next day. Use a de-stress technique (see Chapter 3) if you feel overwhelmed and there is a lot going on.

Acknowledge your accomplishments

Take a couple of minutes to acknowledge what you have accomplished during the day, even if it's not much. It's important to acknowledge yourself for making it through the day. If you are very target driven sometimes it is easy to look at what's next and forget what you got done. Stop this habit. It only buys you a never-ending to-do list. Trust me: I'm a complete task-focused machine. I'm always dissatisfied and looking at the next thing to do. I have to remind myself frequently to acknowledge what I have completed. When I do this it makes a huge difference to my sense of how productive I am.

9 ENJOY THE REST OF THE EVENING

Once you're done with work, enjoy the rest of the evening. In the previous step you completed everything there is to do. You have created a psychological boundary between work and the rest of the day. It will also help not to check any work emails or messages after work. Have fun, do something for yourself, see some loved ones. Do whatever makes you feel great at the end of the day and is legal. This may sound like an obvious point but many people just go home unsatisfied or annoyed and frustrated. Enjoying the rest of the evening acts as a buffer between work and bedtime. You don't want to carry any frustrations further than work and into your evening or, worse, into your sleep. If you feel tired at the end of the workday, use the energising exercises.

10 SLEEP OR REST WELL

Before you go to sleep, take the time to relax. You could have some hot tea, take a bath, or read. Again, avoid computer work, which tends to put your mind into a high-activity state. You will sleep better when you relax. Carrying tension into your sleep can stay with you and prevent you from enjoying a restful night. If you wake up tired or with aches and pains, it's most likely due to not relaxing properly the night before. Use exercises to help you sleep (Chapter 4). Make sure you have a clear head. Again the steps for de-stressing after work will help. However, if anything comes up after work, review it and let it go so you can have a clear head before you sleep. Just as stating your intentions at work is effective, stating an intention of getting a good night's sleep will help you sleep well.

Summary

Use the 10 steps to create an effective day. Starting in the morning feeling great, maintaining the energy and momentum of the day, slowing down to completion at the end of the day: you will finish the day feeling satisfied, with a sense of accomplishment.

- Clear chatter – start the day well.
- Start work with a bang.
- Concentrate – use intentions. Work in bursts.
- Maintain momentum.
- Take lunch.
- Remember to perk up energy.
- End of day.
- De-stress – acknowledge your accomplishments.
- Enjoy rest of the evening.
- Sleep well.

CHAPTER 7

Getting deeper

CONTEXT, ENERGY, STRUCTURES

So far we have looked at how to step out of our default stress cycle and into the energy cycle, how to get better sleep and how the mind makes the difference. Now we are going to delve a bit deeper into what it takes to move into a high performance zone and be more effective in getting things done.

There are many time- and life-management systems out there, and while many are effective at improving time management, they often don't address a vital key to successful performance and productivity. True performance, productivity and satisfaction are dependent on three success factors: **context**, **energy** and **structure**. All three factors need to be in place to ensure lasting effectiveness for work and play. We've covered energy in detail and we've touched upon context to some degree with themes, creating how you want to view the world for the day. Now let's explain it and look at how it all fits together.

The **context** is the big picture, the vision. This is the 'what' you are up to and the 'why' you are up to it. It includes your motivations, your beliefs and how you perceive the world.

The context influences the scope of what is possible in your life. What you are up to will determine how much energy you need and the structure that will help you to reach your goals.

Speak to any successful person and you will notice that they are motivated by empowering beliefs. They are on a mission, working on a big goal or vision. They also have a high level of energy, and they have the systems and structures in place to support them in what they are doing.

If you are the CEO of a multinational company, you will need a lot of energy and the right structures and systems to channel your energy in the right direction. On the other hand, if you work in an unchallenging nine-to-five job, spend the rest of your life watching TV, and just live to enjoy the weekend, you don't need much energy and the systems to support that energy won't be as robust.

Energy is the fuel needed to drive you. It determines the speed at which you get things done or get results and how long you can keep going. When energy is harnessed and channelled, things move efficiently. When energy is lacking or unfocused, getting things done is hard work, results are more difficult to come by and you tend to run out of steam.

Systems and structures are the things that support you in the activities you are engaged in. This includes how your time, your work, your life and your environment are organised. This is a fairly wide category. However, usually you will find you will have most of the necessary systems and structures in place and it is merely an issue of upgrading a system or tweaking it. Structures include your personal time management system, such as your diary and calendar, and move on to the software, technology and other productivity systems you use for support. On a wider level, this includes the people and teams with whom you work – they are your systems for leverage. For example, a junior executive is more likely to have a calendar and access to a secretary, while a CEO will have a personal assistant who effectively handles his or her diary and other support systems. Organisations are usually designed with systems in mind, while individuals have systems that may have developed more spontaneously.

Using a metaphor: if you were embarking on a journey to a far destination, **context** is the map and the route, **systems and structure** comprise the vehicle you use and **energy** is the fuel.

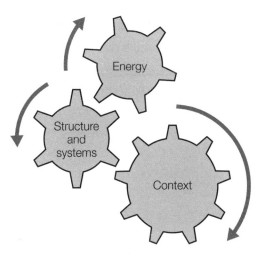

CONTEXT, ENERGY AND SYSTEMS

These three success factors are interdependent. **Context influences your amount of energy**. If you have a great vision and a zest for living, you are more likely to have the energy for the things you want to do. In other words, how you view what you are doing will affect your energy. A daunting or overwhelming project will sap your energy and enthusiasm, as will something that you view as a waste of time. A project that you find inspiring and motivating will enhance your energy. **Structure supports energy**. The type of work you are doing, as well as the amount, will determine the systems and structures that will support you in getting things done.

Having the correct systems in place will help you focus your energy and direction. **Energy helps you move towards your goals; it is the fuel in the tank**. Energy will support you in your systems and structures. For example, when you have a full day in your diary, you will need the necessary energy to manage all of those commitments. People with low energy tend to limit what they do based on how they feel and their perceived energy levels. A period of low energy will have an impact on your context.

This may sound a bit theoretical right now but we will go on to explain this more fully.

CHAPTER 8

The power of perspective

PERSPECTIVE

A gentleman walked past a building site to see three men laying bricks. He approached the first and asked, 'What are you doing?'

Annoyed, the first man answered, 'What does it look like I'm doing? I'm laying bricks!'

He walked over to the second bricklayer and asked the same question.

The second man responded, 'Oh, I'm making a living.'

He asked the third bricklayer the same question, 'What are you doing?'

The third man looked up, smiled, and said, 'I'm building a cathedral.'

This story is a well-known metaphor for how different people view the same job. All three bricklayers are physically doing the same thing, but how they view what they are doing is completely different. Of the three men in the story, one of them has an empowering perspective about what he is doing – helping to build a cathedral. We would expect him to be happier and go farther in life. While he uses the same tools as the other bricklayers, he is more likely to have more energy for life than they do.

How often do we see people in companies just laying bricks or making a living? We could all benefit from upgrading the way we perceive the things we do. For example, imagine if you could borrow Richard Branson's brain for a day and put it into yours. How would 'you' think and act differently? How would you see your job? What opportunities would you see that you didn't see before?

Often when I'm stuck with a problem I identify someone who is successful in that area and either speak to them if I know them or imagine speaking to them. I examine how they view the world and how that makes them successful in their endeavour. For example, I often speak to people who are good at relationships to find out how they view the world and learn how I can change my point of view to have greater success in that area.

It's not common to really consider our personal or organisational perspective on things. We may have a goal or a vision for something, but we don't fully consider our motives for doing what we are doing. In other words, most people don't stop to look at what they are doing.

Our perspective forms part of a larger view of life. The context. Think of the context as the bubble we live in. In *As You Like It* Shakespeare writes that all the world is a stage and we are merely players. As a player in your own story you will have your own goals, perspectives on life and motivations. These come together to form the context within which your story plays. The totality of our context determines why we do what we do and explains all our actions.

So let's define this context a bit. We can break the elements of context down to:

The what – What you are doing; your goal or vision.

The why – Your motives, reasons, or values that drive what you do.

Perspective – How you view what you are up to.

If you go through life with no awareness of this context you can easily go off-track and forget about what's important – what you are really doing and why.

For example, let us take Barack Obama's electoral campaign and victory in the 2008 United States presidential election. **The what** of Barack Obama's context was trying to win the election. **The why** of his context could have been winning the election for personal glory or power, but his context was bigger; he wanted to bring change and hope to America. How about his **perspective**? We could say he views a world where people can come together despite their differences.

This context actually enabled him to create such a successful campaign that it kept him going even when the odds seemed improbable. He was successful in communicating this context to others to such a degree that he managed to reach out to people who had never participated in politics before. Additionally, he employed systems that had never been used before in politics, such as social networking. Even after the election, many organisations and people voluntarily participated on his behalf. Here we see an example of someone with a powerful context.

We can break context into different levels, as shown in the diagram below.

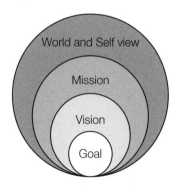

THE ELEMENTS OF CONTEXT

- The global context is determined by our perspective or view of life, our self-image, our perception of reality and our values. We call this the 'World and Self view'.

- The mission is about our personal purpose in life. What we are up to in a specific area.

- A vision is a clear picture of something happening at a defined point or period in time in the future.

- Goals are specific targets or results we want to achieve/have.

We don't walk around defining our context for everything we do in life, but most of us have a default context that constantly runs in the background. Either we have chosen it or (more usually) it has been created for us through our conditioning and experiences in life. It's a good idea and great practice to periodically take the time to define or re-define your context.

Context is not limited to an individual; it can also be organisational. If you look at organisations, most have at least one mission statement, vision statement, or statement of values on their corporate website. Let's look at the context of Google, a successful company.

'Google's **mission** is to organize the world's information and make it universally accessible and useful.' Google's **vision**, which has now been realised, is to be 'widely recognized as the world's largest search engine – an easy-to-use free service that usually returns relevant results in a fraction of a second'.

Context must be maintained and monitored regularly, because you will either drift toward your natural, default context (which is generally not as inspiring as the one you create) or be knocked off course by outside influences to something else which may not be right for you.

When people lose sight of their context, they lose sight of why they are doing what they are doing and hence lose motivation or steer away from their goal. For example, during the 2008 United States presidential election, one could argue that John McCain lost sight of his context in some of the presidential debates. This was clear as he drifted away from his vision for America to a 'win at all costs' type of campaign. His campaign deteriorated into personal attacks on Obama and, as a result, lost a lot of credibility. Context or purpose is similar to a ship crossing the Atlantic from the United Kingdom. If you are just a few degrees off course, you could end up in Mexico when you wanted to go to Miami.

We see this in the corporate world. Most people start off with an idea of where they want to get to or what they'd like to achieve in their careers. They have a 'What' they are up to and the 'Why'. But speak to them a few years into their careers and you can tell they have settled.

Some are on the treadmill of working hard, living in the tunnel of business as usual, but are not connected to the 'What' they are up to and the 'Why'. Just surviving, not enjoying work very much and suffering from stress.

Generally the most successful people are aware of their context, why they are doing what they are doing. Are you?

Or have you forgotten why you are here? Are you existing just to make a living?

THE BIG PICTURE, OR CREATING A PERSONAL CONTEXT

Let's take the time to create or define your own personal context. Creating a context is a rewarding experience. We all have our own unique talents and skills, but when we create or discover our purpose, we really come alive and are able to follow our path to our own personal success.

The first step to creating or rediscovering our context is to look at our lives in perspective. We live in an age in which, due to our knowledge of and access to health care, it is possible to live longer than ever before. If we take good care of ourselves, we are capable of living healthy lives in our senior years and, as a result, the majority of us can achieve a lot more than our grandparents did. Personally, I believe we need to debunk the myth of working until retirement. When people retire and do nothing, they usually die earlier than those who continue to work. A study by Shell indicated that people who retire at 55 are 89% more likely to die in the 10 years after retirement than those who retire at 65. I have met quite a few people who are successfully working in their 70s and beyond. There are many examples of older folks achieving a great deal in their senior years. For example, Buckminster Fuller worked right up until he died at 87, and Hugh Hefner is still enjoying his life in his eighties. Nelson Mandela, in his 90s, is still an inspiring role model and contributor to society. American actress Betty White hosted *Saturday Night Live* at age 88 and, at nearly 89, has a starring role in a new TV sitcom. The global elders, consisting of some of the most inspiring statesmen in the world, are, to me, an indication of what we can become and what we can do well into our old age.

So with a view of our lifetime in mind, let's create.

WORLD AND SELF VIEW

Your view of the world has been in the making for most of your life, from first consciousness and through your upbringing formed by your parents, schools and peers. Your experiences in life have determined your view of the world. As human beings we have created certain beliefs based on our experiences.

While some of these beliefs are beneficial and have been successful in getting you to where you are, some have actually hindered you. I have helped numerous people overcome negative beliefs that have held them back in their relationships, careers and families. To accelerate our success, it is important to examine our limiting beliefs, or our view of the world, and see if they actually do benefit us.

If you could get all of your beliefs out of your head and onto a piece of paper, you would quickly see which ones are beneficial and which ones are not. You would be able to get rid of the ones that are not. Unfortunately, most of our beliefs are hidden from our view, running in the background, and are often difficult to change even when we are aware of them.

We can change these views by first bringing to awareness then questioning ourselves when these beliefs show up. We also might be able to reveal them by working on our personal development or working with a coach. In fact, in life we are either changing our world view proactively, or it gets changed by our environment or life experiences. For example, if you often end up in bad relationships you might find the view that you can't really trust others is working to further hinder your ability to build healthy relationships.

The world view is our view of ourselves, other people and the world around us and our place in it.

Here are some common examples of world views or beliefs that people have:

- Life is hard, and we have to struggle to survive.
- You always have to be number one to succeed.
- It's hard to get a job.
- Only the strong survive.
- It is our responsibility to take care of the planet.
- Everyone can achieve their dreams with enough effort.
- People are fundamentally great.
- People are selfish and self-centred.
- Men are bastards.
- Women can't be trusted.
- People can't be trusted.
- I am the sole architect of my success.
- My life is good but limited.

Whenever you come across stressful or challenging situations, by stopping for a minute and examining your world view and your beliefs you can often gain a new perspective on life and find different ways of dealing with the problem. For example, you are struggling at work to get promoted and you can't seem to convince your bosses and colleagues that you are worthy of a promotion. You realise you have a belief that people can't be trusted. You'll see that because of this belief people find it hard to relate to you. You may be a bit cold with them or falsely charming with them but there is always something 'off' in your relationships with people. They may like you, but they always feel there is some sort of barrier in the way which affects their confidence in you and their perception of you. They may feel that you can't be trusted either. Realising that you have this belief and then changing it can change your career chances overnight. So here is a little spot test to catch your default beliefs.

Exercise

1 Complete the following sentences to gain insight into your view of the world:

'Life is …'
'My life is …'
'People are …'
'The world is …'

2 The next thing is to look at what sort of life a person would have if they had that belief. For example how would life turn out for a person who had the view that they couldn't trust people.

> **3** You can even interview people you know to find out how you come across to them.

YOUR MISSION OR PURPOSE

In my experience from coaching, many people have not sat down to find or create their purpose or mission in life. It took me several years of drifting until I found, or rather decided on, my purpose. That kind of work often needs some coaching or a specific course or seminar. From my experience in coaching, people usually have one of the following types of purpose:

■ **Life purpose**: You are clear on your purpose and are living it. For example, 'My purpose is to ensure that no child goes hungry.' An example would be Bob Geldof. He is clearly living out his life purpose.

■ **Time horizon purpose**: You have a direction for your life and have some goals and objectives for the next 3–10 years. It sounds like: 'I'm not sure what my true life purpose is but for the next 5 years or so I want to work on raising awareness of the environment.'

■ **Right now purpose**: You have a purpose for right now or in the meantime. You can make it up, it doesn't have to be the right thing. It could even be finding your purpose. At some point, you will find or create a new purpose. For example, 'I don't really have a strong sense of purpose, but right now I am helping my organisation double in size and make the difference it does.'

- **Guided purpose**: You are not 100% sure of your purpose but you know you are guided in the direction you need to go in. 'My purpose is to live a life guided by God or the universe.'

- **Living in the now**: You are not worrying about purpose and are just enjoying life as it is and living in the now. Note, this is different from someone who has never considered their purpose. It applies to those who have decided that this is what they are up to for now. 'Right now I am living in the now, enjoying every day as it comes.'

- **Searching for purpose**: You are not sure what your life is about and feel as though you're just drifting with no direction, but you are aware of the problem and are looking at how to find your purpose. 'I don't know what my purpose is; I'm finding it as I go.'

- **No purpose or directionless**: You are not sure what your life is about and feel as though you're just drifting with no direction. 'I don't know what my purpose is, I'm just trying to survive right now.' These people here are likely to get blown around by events and circumstances in their lives.

Having a mission or purpose is not essential; your life will still function well without it. However, in my experience the bigger the game you are playing the more a mission and purpose become useful. This is why most organisations have a mission; they are up to making a big impact on the world. The late Steve Jobs, CEO of Apple, made an excellent speech about finding your purpose.

'Your job is to fill a large part of your life and the only way to be truly satisfied is to do what you believe is great work.

The only way to do great work is to love what you do. If you have not found it yet keep on looking. Do not settle. Like everything that has to do with the heart you will notice when you find it.'

We are not going to do the work on finding or creating a mission as that could take a whole book and at least a whole day of work. Instead we are going to look at a great proxy for creating your mission: the self-image statement.

Self-image statement

A self-image statement is a positive statement of who you are right now; who you are becoming; or who you will be in the future. Creating a self-image statement is about creating a simple motivating mission. It is the equivalent of 'I am building a cathedral' in the story of the three builders. Here are some examples of a self-image statement:

- I am on the path to greatness.
- I am the future CEO of an innovative company.
- When I work collaboratively with others, I make a real difference in this job/organisation/life.
- I'm a great father/mother and contributor to my family.
- I am a relentless leader.
- I am a genius in the making.
- I am going to touch many people's lives, living a life of contribution.
- I am a world traveller, out to explore the planet and have fun.
- I am a warrior of the light.

- I am the one who is going to make a difference here.

- I am going to be the top salesperson in this company.

- I am hot stuff.

You can have a self-image statement that leads to a specific goal such as the future CEO of this company or something more esoteric, like a warrior of the light. Whatever inspires you or lights you up. If you go for a goal-related self-image statement, make it believable for you. It has to be something that you actually want to achieve and are taking action to reach. For example, if you work in the mailroom and tell yourself you are the future CEO of that company, then you had better be working on getting promoted in that organisation in order to get there (which is entirely possible, as has been proved many times over by industry giants such as Disney's Dan Adler and Simon Cowell).

Exercise

Create your own self-image statement that inspires you. It doesn't have to be the right one and you can change it anytime you want. You can keep your statement for a day, a week, or a year. Do whatever resonates for you. If you think your goal is too ambitious, just allow yourself to take longer to get there. For example, if you aspire to be the CEO of a company and you are working in the mailroom, would it be possible to become CEO in 10 or 20 years? You'll know when you have the right self-image statement, because it will resonate with you and motivate you.

If you start the day with a self-image statement, how does your day begin to look?

Now that you have started to define a bit of your context, how does your life look? What actions can you take to make your life look differently? How do you start to act? How does your current life fit into that context?

For example, when I experience a setback, I look at it as one of the obstacles on the way to becoming a great leader in life.

Vision and goals

A **vision** is a clear picture of your life or an organisation at a defined point or period in the future. For example, in five years' time I will have been promoted to division head; I will be happily married in a nice penthouse in central London. Or, for an organisation, in five years' time we will be the most visited website in the world.

Goals are specific targets or results you want to achieve. For example, get a promotion by the end of the year with at least a 5% pay rise. Most of us automatically create goals or projects. If you don't find yourself getting to where you want to be, consider looking at the goals that you are setting and set ones that motivate you.

Summary

■ We have looked at how the context of your perspective, beliefs and motivations influences your life and how
we can change elements of our context to have a more
inspiring life.

■ Take some time to do the exercises to examine your world
view, your mission, your vision and your goals.

CHAPTER 9

Let's get practical – systems and structures

SYSTEMS AND STRUCTURES

We've looked at how the way you think about what you have to do influences what there is to do and we've dealt with having the energy to get everything done. So now we are energised up and we know what we are doing, let's get practical and look at the third success factor – systems and structures. Your systems and structures are the 'How' you get things done, the tools you use to get things done. Adding the right systems and structures to put in action what you plan gives you a powerful strategy for success.

The dictionary definition of a system is: 'A set of detailed methods, procedures, and routines established or formulated to carry out a specific activity, perform a duty, or solve a problem.'

There are so many systems out there that it is just a matter of picking the right system for you. You will be aware of software tools and processes that work for your business or industry. The considerations you will need are ease of use, time required to learn, time required to maintain and the usefulness of it. If your system is not working, find one that does works.

STRUCTURES

Definition of structure

Structure is the organisation we give to our lives or our time. Just as a glass holds liquids, our structure holds our way of life together.

The dictionary definition of structure is 'something arranged in a definite pattern of organisation'.

To tailor that a bit, let's refine the definition to 'the organisation that we put in place to support us in our goals and commitments.'

We will usually have a default way of organising our lives (or not) that works to a certain extent. The power of structures really comes into play when you have lots of things you want to manage or some key goals you want to achieve. By examining the existing structures you are using you can find changes that allow you to achieve more. Examples of where structures are useful: finding time to exercise when you work too many hours; finding the time to spend with your children when you have a demanding job. Generally the busier you are, or the more important your goals are, the more structure you will need.

There are four key factors to structure:

1 How your day is structured, how your time is used and the constraints on your time.

2 Your commitments and agreements.

3 Your physical environment.

4 The people around you.

Almost everyone has a structure to some degree. Most working people's lives are automatically structured by their jobs and other commitments outside of work. Another example is that stay-at-home mothers usually structure their lives around their children's routines. The best way to understand the power of structure is to look at some examples of how different jobs have different structures. Understanding the structures we already have allows us to adapt and change them so that they can best serve what we are up to.

EXAMPLES OF STRUCTURES

CASE STUDY

Trader in an investment bank

If you are a trader, your structure is determined by the trading hours of the market in which you operate and the team with which you work. Your **timetable** is determined by the markets, and your **commitment**

▶

is to trade profitably and be able to do that in a timely manner. Your **environment**, your trading desk and the trading floor, is set up for you to be able to do this easily. You also have relevant computer systems to be able to do this. In effect, your structure at work (which has an impact on your whole life) is set up for you to react to the markets. When you are at work, what you can do is limited by your need to be near your desk, ready to trade during market hours. You may have to start work at 7am and go to bed earlier than your friends outside of work, and you won't be able to attend much to your personal life during working hours. You also may not be able to get away from your desk for lunch.

Teachers

If you are a teacher in a school, the structure of your job is set by the school **timetable**, your teaching timetable and the class **environment**. Your **commitment**, or job description, is to teach the children in your class according to a curriculum. The curriculum is often mapped out in advance, so classrooms are structured around the curriculum. There is limited freedom in the structure. If you are teaching in the classroom, you can't do administrative work while you are standing in front of a captive and hopefully captivated audience. Also, your holidays must be taken outside of the school term.

Similarly, a consultant doctor's structure is determined by the patients he needs to see, any emergencies that arise, and whether or not he is on call.

The above examples are quite structured jobs. Here are some more examples with more freedom in the creation of the structure.

People who create their own structure

Project managers create structures to work on and complete their projects. They create **commitments** for themselves and others, and they create teams, **environments** and project **timetables**. In addition, they manage other people, schedule meetings and track the progress of their projects.

Successful students create structures by which they pass their exams. They create a **timetable** of study. They work in a library or some other **environment** that is suitable to them, and they may create or join study groups or get a study partner.

People who own their own business or work for themselves may have a more flexible **timetable**, which is influenced by client appointments and opportunities to grow the business. Their **commitments** may include more personal commitments as well as professional ones. For example, they may create a structure that enables them to be home by 5pm to spend time with their family. Their **environment** may be an office or their home, or even a small or large team.

Therefore, we can see how our work provides a certain structure. Many people don't need to create their own structure for work if their existing one works well. Others may just need to tweak their structures a bit to make other areas of their lives work better.

THE ELEMENTS OF STRUCTURE

The main elements of structure are:

Your timetable

This is the way your time is set up – how your time is influenced, externally, by your job or your need to do something at a certain time (e.g. pick up kids from school at 3pm), and internally, by your need to get up at 7am to go to the gym before work. This also includes recurring practices that you do daily or weekly.

Your environment

This is how your physical environment is set up (e.g. your desk, your home, your company) for your work, and includes which environments you need to do certain tasks.

Your commitments or agreements

The commitments or agreements that you follow or put in place e.g. your job description, your commitment to get and stay fit, the need to look after a relative, or to progress meetings that you set up.

Other people

The people you work with, look after, or interact with; the people who can support you in your endeavour.

USING STRUCTURES

A structure can be used in any area of your life or for a specific goal. We will look at some examples.

The first step is to define your goal. For example, lose half a stone in two months.

Next answer these questions:

- **Timetable**: When are you going to do it? What days and what times? Are there any adjustments to be made?
- **Environment**: Where is the best place to do it? Do you need to make any modifications to your environment?
- **Commitments** or agreements: Are there any commitments or agreements you have already in place or can you put some in place?
- **People**: Are there any other people involved?

So if your goal is to lose half a stone in two months, the environments that will probably help you will include the gym plus your home with all junk food removed and replaced with healthy food. The commitment would be to do exercises at specific times. Other people involved could be a personal trainer or other people to work out with.

If your goal is to get a promotion, your structure may include regular meetings with a mentor (timetable and people), a plan to work on the skill sets you want to develop (commitments). For example, if you need to be more confident in public speaking, you might attend a speaking class, obtain some leadership coaching or set up weekly update presentations. You may want to modify your job description (agreements).

I once consulted with a director who had a hectic social life and worked long hours. He had a concern about eating healthily as he often had to go out for drinks late into the evening and as a result didn't have much sleep or have time to get decent food. He would frequently go without lunch. This was a problem for him as he didn't feel healthy and was tired at the weekend. So his goals were: 1 To eat more healthily; 2 To make a minor adjustment to his lifestyle to have time to exercise and still be able to socialise. The challenging factor was to take small convenient steps so that it wouldn't feel like a big effort.

A structure that would work for him is to have his personal assistant set up a regular takeaway order for him at lunchtime from a healthy food company. He could also hire a personal trainer who would pick him up from the office and ensure that he trained.

ADAPTING STRUCTURES AT WORK

Often, we don't realise that we can take control over our existing structure in order for it to work better for us. For example, at work we can set up times when we can't be interrupted, co-opt a meeting room to get peace and quiet, or move regular meetings to another day. In addition, we may need to bring structure into our personal lives to have more time for ourselves. Structures that will give us more free time at the weekends may include doing household chores in the morning or evening during the week, doing laundry on Thursdays, or hiring external help.

If you run your own business, you may have complete freedom regarding how you run your business, or you may be constrained by the hours of operation of your customers, or by personal commitments, such as looking after children. Instead of adopting a nine-to-five structure, you may create something else that works for you, incorporating your commitments outside of work. Below are some elements of structure that you can take on in various areas of life.

Structure for productivity at work

- Have a tidy desk, so you'll know where everything is.
- Use a calendar that works for you. Ensure that it is full enough to call you into action, but not so packed that you become overwhelmed.
- Take regular breaks.
- Create transition periods in your day so that you rejuvenate for each activity.
- Schedule your most productive time for your most worthwhile activities.
- Have weekly update meetings so that everyone has specific deadlines to work to.
- Have a project manager or project management system.
- Be accountable to someone so that you stay on track.
- Appoint someone to check your work.
- Create a checklist for routine items.
- Set aside a daily practice time to get you in a productive frame of mind. This may include jogging, yoga, deep breathing, reading and praying, spending time with your children, or washing the dishes. This can be something small, which takes about 10 minutes, or it can be something longer.

For health and fitness

- Make time to go to the gym.

- Keep a fitness progress sheet.

- Have your personal trainer visit you to make sure you do your exercises.

- Jog in the morning so that you get out of the house and start your day with a clear head.

- Cycle to work to get your daily exercise.

- Clear your home of all unhealthy food.

- Keep your food supplements where you can find them easily.

Relationships

- Have a weekly 'date night'.

- Spend time with friends at weekends.

- Speak daily with a friend or loved one so you feel connected. This is particularly useful if you spend a lot of time working by yourself.

- Have a dinner party once a month with friends.

Finances

- Do a weekly or monthly financial review.

- Have a direct debit set up to put money into your savings account.

Personal

- Set up a weekly review of your personal and professional goals.

- Create a challenge or goal for the month.

Peace of mind/wellbeing

- Book a holiday.
- Book a weekly spa treatment.

Structures that don't work or create limited productivity

There are certain structures that don't work for us, or limit our productivity. It often pays to look at our existing structures to determine what doesn't work so we can change them. Here are some structures that limit our productivity:

- Having an open door (or open-door policy if you don't have an office) when you are in a high-interruption or crowded environment.
- Having your email set up so that it interrupts you at inconvenient times (Blackberry users take note).
- Having the internet on, when you know you are prone to distraction.
- Having too a rigid structure when you know you thrive on variety.
- Having no structure when you need to have order and be organised.
- Doing everything on your own when you thrive on being with people or working in teams.
- Having no structure to contain/limit work time, resulting in work expanding to fill the space.

Exercise

This exercise will help you look at your life and bring structure to certain areas:

1 Think of an area of your life that is important to you where you are dealing with a problem. This could be work, health, relationships, or finances.

2 What works about this current area?

3 What elements of your current structure make this area work? (Consider how your time is structured, how your environment is structured, what your commitments are, and the people in your life.)

4 What doesn't work in this area?

5 What elements of your current structure do not work (timetable, environment, people and commitments)?

6 How could you optimise your current structure to improve this area?

7 What other elements of structure could you include – time (daily, weekly, monthly), environment, commitment, other people (join a team, have a buddy to call you to account for your participation, etc.).

CASE STUDY

Vivian works as a lawyer in a large law firm. Her work is client-led and deal-focused, so her workload is determined by what deals she is working on at any given time. There is always clearly defined work to do, and she has some awareness of the work that is coming in.

What doesn't work are the gaps in her day, during which she is not being productive and is waiting for others to finish their work, which often results in the main bulk of the work being done after 5pm.

The changes she could make to her structure are to use the unproductive times to go to the gym, get a massage, do further study, or do some important yet not urgent work that will fulfil her long-term goals. Other things to do could be system maintenance to improve productivity. She could also do something that switches her into a more relaxed state so that she can gear herself up for the main rush.

Tom runs his own business producing widgets with a part-time staff of three people. What works about his work structure is that he can work any hours he wants. His only constraint is that he must be available to answer the phone when the secretary has a day off.

Tom hasn't fully optimised his structure. He could have worked any way he wanted to, but he decided to opt for a nine-to-five timetable because it worked for him in the past. What doesn't work is that his afternoons are not very productive, as he has a lull in his energy levels in the afternoon and doesn't concentrate very well.

Also, Tom hasn't structured the other areas of his life, so his work tends to overrun regularly, and his life is a bit out of balance.

▶

What would make Tom's life more productive would be to figure out what work he could do in the afternoon that takes advantage of his lull in energy and attention and then schedule that work into his calendar and set himself up to be able to do that work.

Tom then needs to look at the other areas of his life and create structures that work in those areas.

Summary

We have looked at how structure can influence our productivity and help us handle the commitments we have in life.

The busier we are the more we will need structure to be able to handle our various commitments.

There are four elements of structure: timetable, environment, commitments and people. By considering all of the elements we can create a structure to help us achieve any goal.

Next, we will look at tools for productivity!

CHAPTER 10

The element of time

PRINCIPLES

Now that we have looked at how structures can make a difference in our lives let's look more closely at how we can master the first element of structure: time

Time is one of the most precious and abundant resources we have. Effective use of it makes the difference between achievement and failure. This chapter presents some useful tips and tools to master the use of our time, creating greater productivity and satisfaction and less stress.

Have you ever heard the saying, if you want to get something done give it to a busy person? Why is that? A busy person has a different relationship to time: they not only use it wisely but are able to extract more value from the time they have. Have you heard the saying, time flies when you are having fun? That is because when you are enjoying yourself or have intense focus all the other stuff is off your mind. When your mind is focused on what you are doing you'll find you are more productive and will get more done.

Managing time is really a matter of managing focus. We've talked about how the mind focuses; here we will use practical tools and tips to aid your focus.

When we do not focus ourselves effectively we are bombarded with interruptions not only from other people but also from distracting thoughts unrelated to your present activity. They can pop up at anytime, just like those nuisance email alerts (switch them off right now). It could be when you are in the middle of pulling together your departmental budget and suddenly find yourself thinking that you must do your own tax return. Or you are in a meeting about the future strategy of the business and the nagging thought that you must remember to post your brother's birthday card persistently interrupts your thinking.

Just like email alerts, you need to switch these time invaders off, and the tools presented in this chapter have been designed to do just that so that you can focus on what you are doing and tune out everything else that is not relevant for you right now.

CALENDAR – THE MOST IMPORTANT TOOL

The essential tool for managing your time and creating structure is your calendar. Now, I suspect you are thinking that this is hardly revolutionary; but hold on. I'm willing to bet that, like many people, you are simply using your calendar to record meetings and appointments. This is a big under-utilisation of a much more powerful tool. When we start to use our calendars as accurate representations of how we spend our time and how we plan for things in the future, we gain more clarity, more control over our lives and have more peace of mind.

Parkinson's Law states that work expands to fill the time available. We've all been in the situation of having a lot of time to do a project only to be rushing in the end to get it all done; and we've had the experience of turning a piece of work around in record time. To make effective use of this principle, give yourself the minimum amount of time needed to finish a piece of work with a bit of safety margin. Here is where the calendar comes into use with Parkinson's Law.

Think of your calendar as a time budgeting or planning tool. Just as a financial budget must be a correct representation of your present financial situation and your financial plans if it is to work, your calendar must have the same status and be a truly representative picture of how you intend to use your time. Unscheduled time tends to get filled with busy work. When used properly, a calendar will help you handle productively any project or activity you are working on.

THE RULES TO MAKE FULL USE OF YOUR CALENDAR

1 **Your calendar must be an accurate reflection of how you will spend your time**. Everything that is impor-
    tant to you that needs to be done must be scheduled
    in your calendar. If it is not in your calendar, consider

that you haven't really indicated a true intention to get it done, which means it may not get done. The only exception is for small items of less than 15 minutes. These can be batched up into a larger time slot so that it is more workable.

2   **Take time to plan your days and weeks**. Obviously, the main advantage in the use of your calendar is in planning your time; however, a common pitfall for many busy people is putting lots of appointments into the diary without thinking of how the day will go.

   ■ **Mental walk-through**. When you plan, think through or mentally walk through how your day(s) will go and look out for anything that doesn't work for you. For example, schedule important work for when you are more alert, or avoid scheduling important work after a meeting you think will overrun or will be exhausting. On days when you have a lot to do, planning accurately helps you to get related to the reality of what you are doing and how long it will take. Often, people end up working late because they haven't prepared their calendar well enough. They haven't mentally walked through their schedule. When you get into the habit of scheduling your time, you usually know when you will be working late in advance, and then you have some degree of choice over it.

   The planning stage of your calendar is the opportunity to get an overview of your time before committing to it. If you have a large workload and constantly work long hours, you can see whether your planning will allow for a more efficient schedule or if you can use other measures.

■ **When to plan your day**. The best time to plan is the night before, as you've just completed the day's work and have a sense of what needs to be carried over. Reviewing or adjusting your day in the morning is useful if you have had any creative insights overnight or if any urgent matters come up.

3 **Get rid of to-do lists**. To-do lists are good for getting things out of your head and on to paper. The problem with them is that they are not set in a specific time frame, and as such there is no certainty about when you can get them done.

When you have a to-do list you know what you need to do but there is an uncertainty in the back of your mind about how long the items on the list will take you to complete and when you will actually finish the list. The more items on the to-do list the more this rings true. By taking the items off your to-do list and scheduling them, you eliminate the niggling uncertainty and reacquaint yourself with the reality of how long your work will take you.

Other reasons for not using to-do lists is that they tend to grow day by day. When you get to the end of the day there is an overflow for the next day which, rather than giving you a sense of accomplishment from completing your calendar, makes you focus on the things you haven't done. Only use lists to keep track of things that need to be done initially. Schedule items from your list into your diary with the amount of time it will actually take you to do each one. If the items will take less than 15 minutes, batch them up into one time slot. This helps create clarity and peace of mind.

4   **Use alerts for time-critical items**. For all items that are time-critical, include an alert or alarm that will let you know when to do an item. If you have an electronic diary system this is usually automatic. Keeping an alert for non-time-critical items is optional but doing so will help you keep to time. You may want to turn off alerts for non-critical items so your mind doesn't go numb to alerts through having too many. If you use a paper diary, I recommend setting alarms in your mobile phone to alert you. I have coached many people who, although they check their diaries regularly and anticipate appointments, end up late for their appointments because they got distracted at the last minute by something else.

5   **Even if an item is flexible put it in a schedule**. Obviously, some items don't need to be done at specific times. Usually these are put on to-do lists and often get missed or carried over to the next day(s). The power of scheduling these items is in increasing the likelihood of getting them done. It is not important when you do it as long as you allow time and space for the item. Schedule flexible items for when you are likely to do them, but designate them in a way that lets you know they will get done. Often, flexible items end up on a to-do list and then don't get done.

6   **Create a relationship with your calendar by reviewing it often**. Make your calendar your best friend. Even if you have an electronic diary that alerts you to what you are doing, it still pays to review your calendar so that you get some peace of mind and certainty about your day. Review your calendar at least twice a day. Ideally, review it when you have completed each task. Delete completed items or shade in a colour that signifies that item

as 'completed,' just as you would tick off an item on your to-do list.

7   **Break up large tasks and schedule them to maintain productivity**. When working on large projects, it doesn't seem to be worth the effort to schedule anything, as you know what you will be working on over the next few days or weeks. You might have an outline of what you are doing with some estimation of timing, but unless you are highly organised, this can be a recipe for lower productivity as you will miss out on the sense of urgency and self-imposed deadlines that scheduling gives you. Chunking a project down and scheduling the elements as appointments in your calendar helps keep you focused and on-track.

8   **Don't forget to schedule breaks and in-between times**. One of the main stumbling blocks in scheduling is a lack of realism. When you schedule tasks back-to-back and don't take breaks into account while moving between appointments or interruptions, you will tend to go off-track, get behind on your schedule, and spend time trying to catch up. Over time, you will start to think that scheduling doesn't work and give up the notion that you can ever be productive. By taking into account the little items such as breaks, interruptions and conversations in your schedule, you will get a realistic picture of what you are doing and where your time will go. Schedule your rest breaks, lunch breaks and any travel time to meetings. By scheduling these things, you plan your day more effectively. For example, say you are planning to travel to a meeting at 1pm. Normally you would set a reminder to leave for that meeting. But by actively

scheduling the travel time, your mind has more clarity on what you are doing.

9   **For calls and meetings, include preparation and follow-up**. We have all turned up late to meetings because we didn't allow enough time to get there or we didn't anticipate overrun time. Even calls require a bit of preparation time. Allocate preparation time as well as time in your calendar to travel for meetings or prepare for calls. This eliminates the stress of finding out travel details just before you leave the office or searching for phone numbers when your call is due. Scheduling for travel includes having accurate travel information, departure times and leaving some time to grab some coffee on the way.

10 **Allow for emergencies and unplanned activities**. How often do you have days that do not go according to plan? Often, every day? Once a week? How often do you schedule a day hoping that nothing will interrupt your beautifully laid plans? Incorporating some buffer time for interruptions and derailments to your day will set you up to win. If there are no emergencies, you can always do other work during the buffer time. Estimate how much of your time is dedicated to unscheduled calls or interruptions, and schedule these for when they are most likely to occur. Initially, you will probably over- or underestimate your buffer time, but you can refine this as your experience develops.

11 **Get into the habit of scheduling**. When to-do tasks come your way, schedule them immediately. If you can't schedule them instantly, make a note on your pad, PDA/Smartphone, tablet or whatever device you use. There are several advantages of instant scheduling. First, it saves you the hassle of having to remember to do things later

on, and second, it eliminates the risk of things slipping through the net. As to-do items come up, decide when you will be likely to deal with them and schedule a time to do so.

If you regularly need to follow up on meetings or requests, set up a weekly review slot and add items into this slot as you go through the week. If you have an electronic calendar such as Outlook, you can put the items into the notes section of the appointment. If you are using a paper diary and don't have space in the diary for all the items, you can add those items onto a separate list which goes with that time slot.

For example, whenever I go to meetings in the evening, I have a follow-up appointment in my PDA for the next day to do all the things that came up during the evening and to review any notes or actions I need to take. During the course of the evening, I enter all the things I will follow up on into the appointment, and I update this appointment as I go along.

12 **Keep only one calendar**. Keep the same calendar for your work and your life. There really is no separation of work and play when it comes to your life. It is all a reflection of how you allocate your time. Managing two calendars divides your attention and increases the complexity of time management. If you have a work calendar that is accessible to others, use the privacy function for your personal items. If you can't do this you'll have to sync the two calendars or keep one for after hours and one for business, which can be a bit trickier.

TASKS

There are some things you want to do which are not time-critical. To save space and time in your calendar, you can designate these non-time-critical items as tasks.

Keep tasks on simple lists and review periodically to either do or schedule. The only rule for tasks is that they cannot be time-critical; if an item is sitting on a task list and hasn't been done, there should be no consequence to it not getting done. If there are consequences, then schedule the task in your calendar. You can distinguish a task from a critical item by determining the consequence of it not getting done. If there is a consequence, schedule it. If there is no significant consequence, keep it on a task list. Microsoft Outlook has inbuilt tasks which can be dragged into your calendar. If you are using a paper diary, simply make another list for designated tasks. Obviously, this is a to-do list, but the mental designation you give it makes it important.

SIMPLICITY OUT OF COMPLEXITY

How do you feel when you start the day with massive to-do lists that you know you have no chance of actually getting done? And how do you feel when you have an email inbox of 200 unread messages and you are being pinged every two minutes with a new one? Understandably, you probably feel daunted and maybe a little anxious.

To reduce the daunting nature of the things you have to do, simplify them. Simple systems are easier to understand. When we have more simplicity, our minds have less distraction.

Even when we have a lot to do, we can still only pay attention to one thing at a time. Therefore, we only need to have our attention on what we are doing, with a level of reassurance that we have capacity to do the important things we need to do today.

By representing the things we have to do more simply, we can ease some of our mental burdens. Note that we aren't simplifying our work, just how the work appears in our calendar.

The main areas where we need simplicity are in our email systems and calendars. We are not going to touch on email here, as there are plenty of systems out there for dealing effectively with it. The main principle is to keep your inbox for new messages only and empty your inbox daily. We will look at creating a simplified calendar.

By simplifying our calendar and making it appear easier on the eye, we can feel more in control of our schedules.

Consider that your calendar is part of your workspace; make it look tidy and inviting.

SIMPLIFYING YOUR CALENDAR

We have looked at fully scheduling your time in your calendar; now, let's look at the representation. If you are trying to navigate from town A to town B, the design of the map you use will determine how easy it is for you to get from A to B. A colour map will be easier to use than a black and white map, and a map that highlights the route will be even easier to read. The easier something is to read the less figuring out your brain has to do.

Similarly, a neat calendar is easier to use than a chaotic-looking calendar dotted with multiple appointments.

We want to simplify the appearance of our calendar to create an appealing schedule that will help us get from the beginning of the day to the end productively and with minimal stress.

I created the slot method as a useful, easy method for scheduling.

The principle of the slot method is to divide each day into a few large time slots. These time slots represent blocks of achievement where you can do meaningful work. The number of slots can vary between three and six, depending upon the nature of your work and how you want your calendar to be displayed. Time slots can be any length, but to be useful they need to be at least 1.5 hours. A three-slot day, which is the easiest to view, corresponds to a morning, afternoon and evening. A six-slot day divides each of those slots into two. So you get early morning, late morning, beginning of the afternoon, late afternoon and two evening slots.

The slot is a unit of productive time and an opportunity to complete something significant. These units do not include break times or transition periods.

The slots are a way of representing your day, but this doesn't mean that the work you do must take up the whole slot; you can schedule any amount of work into a slot. For example, if your morning slot is three hours, you can schedule four 15-minute items and two one-hour items. Avoid scheduling a lot of 15-minute tasks, as it is harder to get into a rhythm when you look at your calendar and see a whole list of things to do. Put smaller tasks together into 30-minute blocks or, even better, one-hour slots. Of course, if you have a specific appointment during the day that will take 15 minutes, you need to show this. You just want to avoid anything that reads like a to-do list. The idea is to be productive, not busy. Small items give us a sense of busyness, but large blocks give us a sense of accomplishment and thoughtful planning.

Remember, each slot is for productive work. Avoid filling your slots with routine or unproductive work unless it is something small compared to the main bulk of work. If you want to spend a lot of time on admin then create an admin slot.

Leave time at the end of each slot to finish or round up what you have been working on so that you finish it with a sense of achievement.

STRUCTURING YOUR TIME

The slot method is great for planning out the future. If you schedule out into the future all of your slots as blank appointments, then when it comes to scheduling work, you will feel more compelled to put something meaningful into the blank slots. In an electronic calendar, you can set up recurring appointments in the future. (Once you are in the habit of planning by using the slot system, you won't need to keep the recurring appointments.)

Planning this way is also great for ensuring work–life balance. I created the slot system when I was working in a job where I had quite a lot of leeway in planning my activities. The one thing I found was that without any scheduled activities after work, I would end up working late, just going home, having dinner and watching TV. By using the slot method, I felt more obliged to fill my evenings with things that were more fun.

Exercise

Get a blank calendar (you can get one by visiting the energy equation website **www.energyequationbook. com/resources**). You can get a pre-generated three- or six-slot day or create your own. Now fill in the slots that are already weekly occasions. For example, if you play tennis every Sunday at 10am fill this in as a slot. What do you see you have left?

Loads of free time!

By looking at the slots you get an idea of how much free time you have. There are five evenings in the week of non-work time where you have three to six hours per day. You can fill this time by relaxing, spending time with your family, going out to dinner, movies, etc. You can also actually 'choose' to work late!

When you start to add up that time, those five evenings a week correspond to 15 to 30 hours per week to do what you want.

If you add the weekends, which would be another 36 hours (or an additional 6–12 slots), you get 50 to 66 hours a week of leisure time! There are a lot of projects you could do in that time, such as learn a language, write a book, etc. The main thing is to ensure that you have the energy to do these things. Can you see how energy management now becomes important? There is a whole area of life you could miss out on if you don't have enough energy.

Structuring your slots

Creating structure with your slots will help you maximise the use of your time and the activities you want to do. I have a regular schedule which consists of several types of slots during the week. This way, I ensure I make full use of my evenings. Designate slots that are important to you. Here are some examples:

■ Relax slot or night.

■ Date slot (date night).

■ Personal growth slot or study night.

■ Spending time with family slot.

■ Socialising slot.

■ Work late slot.

■ Cinema slot.

■ Exercise slot.

Example of calendar

	Mon	Tues	Wed	Thurs	Fri	Sat	Sun
AM						Chores	Relax
PM						Family	Family
Evening	Seminar	Free	Football	Exercise	Social	Social	Dinner

Creating boundaries

Using the slot system will force you to create boundaries between work and life. Start scheduling your evenings with an activity, even if it is just going home. Scheduling a slot helps you psychologically demarcate time for yourself and you actively use the Parkinson's Law.

USING COLOUR FOR TIME MANAGEMENT

Just as a colour map is better than a black and white one, a calendar with colours helps you to see more easily, at a glance, exactly how your time is allocated. By using specific colours for different items or categories of appointment or work, you can see where you are spending your time and where you may be out of balance. The colour scheme you employ will depend on how you want to measure your time. For example, if you run your own business and want to measure revenue-generating work and you designate that in blue, when you look ahead you will know how much such work you are doing that week by how much blue is in your schedule.

Designate each type of work with a colour. You can base it on your job type or your life balance. For example:

- **Executive**: managing others, meetings, key projects, career critical, relationship building.
- **Life balance**: work, family, friends, travel, vacations, purpose/career development.
- **Banking**: pitching, execution, follow-up, long-term planning, learning.
- **Salesperson**: client visits, prospecting, closing, admin, calls, presentations.

USING COLOUR FOR TIME MANAGEMENT

- **Business owner function model**: sales, marketing, finance, maintenance, leisure, production/operation.

- **Project manager**: specific projects, leisure, meetings, calls, follow-up.

- **E-myth model**: technician work, manager, entrepreneur.

Below is a simple colour system, based on business work, meetings, personal, routine items, critical meetings and vacations (there are more examples on **www.energy equationbook.com/resources**).

In this case, the slots were already set up in advance, and the new appointments were scheduled the day before.

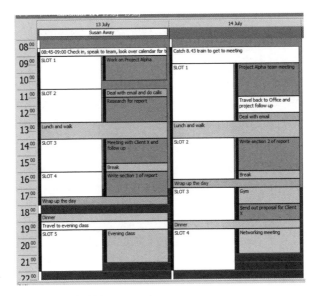

SIMPLE COLOUR SYSTEM

Using these simple calendar techniques will significantly improve your productivity and peace of mind. The more certainty you have, the more you will feel in control of your life.

Now that we've covered the importance of using your calendar and how to structure your time using the slot system, not only will you find yourself more productive, you will also have more free time for yourself.

Longer term planning

Most of what we have done so far is day-to-day, week-to-week planning. But life can be boring when our days are the same old routine. Planning for the longer term is a matter of zooming out and looking at the year. You can divide the year into quarters or even months and start at any point.

During the year we need points in time when we recharge our batteries, so schedule some relaxation, recovery and fun.

Let's take a step back and look at the year in terms of the months and quarters. Now add in the holidays or breaks you are going to have. I recommend a long weekend break of five days in total (including the weekend) at least once a quarter. Then allocate your vacation days as makes sense to you with the view of having sufficient rest and recovery time.

Quarter 1	Quarter 2	Quarter 3	Quarter 4
Jan 1 long w/e	Apr 1 long w/e	Jul	Oct
Feb	May	Aug 2 x long w/e	Nov 1 long w/e
Mar	Jun 1 long w/e	Sep 10-day break	Dec 10-day break

By looking at your year in this view it allows you to see what rest points you are creating for yourself

---

Exercise

1 Create a bucket list. Write down a list of 50 things you want to do, places you want to visit or things you want to experience.

2 When you've written those down, pick a few from the list and plan them in your calendar. Make sure you have them spaced out sufficiently in time.

CHAPTER 11

A whole new world

At this point you have all the tools you need to help you to live a life of increasing energy. You know how to get better sleep, how stress affects our energy and how to de-stress: how you can use the power of your thoughts to focus and concentrate better and be more productive. You know how to get into the zone. You know how the way you view life affects your experience of life and how effective you are in all areas of life. You know how to create structures to support that effectiveness. All that is left now is to practise.

What does this allow?

A more fulfilling life packed with the things you want to do and the end of stress! Maybe a stress-free life seems a bit too ideal. Our stress mechanism is an automatic reaction so there will always be an initial pull to react to stressful situations, but using what is contained in this text will allow you to eliminate stress much earlier, before it has a negative impact on your body and mind.

You now know how to get more effective sleep. Getting good sleep is as much psychological as it is physical. If you want to maximise your sleep it is important to focus on being relaxed and creating the right bedtime routine so that you go to bed relaxed. It is equally important not to worry about the occasional bad night's sleep; deep breathing and energy exercises can relieve some of the problems of not sleeping.

You now know how to get more energy. This is where the real payoff is. The more you practise the energy exercises and master them, the more benefit you'll see in your life: from getting rid of stress-related symptoms such as headaches to improving to preventing long-term illnesses.

You now know how to master your mind and use it to get into the zone: the time and space where we are focused, concentrated and where we lose all sense of time. This is increasingly important in the world of work as we are in an age where there is just too much information. Being able to filter, focus and concentrate allows us to continue to be effective in a maelstrom of information. Too much distraction scatters your attention and leaves you not only less effective but confused and out of sorts. Actively taking the time to tame your wandering mind and focus will allow you to be more effective and give you peace of mind.

These are the benefits you are now able to enjoy:

Better performance at work. When you can get into the zone you will get a lot more work done than when you are stressed. You also make better decisions when at ease instead of stressed. When you have more energy not only will you perform better but you'll have a more positive influence on others. People notice your energy and it has a subtle but powerful influence on others.

In organisations, this allows people to experience being healthy, vital and focused, bringing all of themselves to work, reducing sick days, increasing employee satisfaction and company performance.

Just as important, you'll find yourself having more time and energy outside of work to do the things you enjoy. Also you will feel more present. When you are free of stress and demands on your attention, you will have more energy and attention for the present. People notice when you're present with them and when you're not.

What will you do with this information?

Originally I wrote this text for those who want to push the envelope and increase performance: the type of people who would rather get more done than waste time sleeping. My attitude has changed now. I'm more balanced. I'm still about achievement but I believe we need to work in harmony with our bodies. Yes, we can push our body to perform, but I believe working with where your body is now and coaxing rather than forcing is a better method. In other words, I believe in productivity with wellbeing and my view towards productivity is more about accomplishment than just doing work for work's sake. Despite that, what has been covered will allow you to push the envelope in terms of performance. If you are in a job or lifestyle where the opportunity for sleep is limited, you will be able to make the most of the sleep you have.

Create work–life balance: The more effective you are at work the more you are able to get done in the available time. This allows you to have more balance in life; more time for you and for your family.

Access your genius: Our bodies and minds have an innate genius, our cells regenerate to the extent that we have a new body every 5–7 years, our body breathes by itself, it knows how to fight off infection and disease. The mind also has a positive influence over the body, as seen with the power of the placebo; who knows what else is possible? With the energy exercises and by harnessing the power of the mind we briefly delved into neuroscience and energy practices such as yoga, tai chi and meditation. These are practices that have been scientifically proven to make important changes in the body. For example, meditation increases the density of the frontal lobe. Energy exercises have been shown to promote self-healing. The practices in this book provide a stepping stone for accessing more of your genius.

Implementation: Where should you start? Some people like to dive in. Some people like to put the structure in first and allow small changes. Some people like to create the context first.

Create a structure: The easiest thing to do is to put in a practice in the morning to do energy exercises. Schedule this to make it easier.

OVERCOMING OBSTACLES

So you have the key to having it all; let's look at what might get in your way. I know, as with any text, some people will take these concepts and fly with them. Some will forget and some will implement a few things but not the whole. Let's look at what might get in the way of implementing the practices.

CASE STUDY

Alison worked in a hectic environment as a management consultant. She had a very demanding job, and her co-workers expected a lot from her. Alison started off well, but when her department went through a reorganisation she started to get stressed while trying to deal with all the new demands. Her workload increased due to the reorganisation, which highlighted Alison's underlying belief that she had to get everything done and that she could not say no to anything (according to her beliefs about herself). She became a victim to the demands of the job and could no longer see the forest for the trees. All she could see were constant demands. She became defensive and irritable when she was asked to do something, and she constantly felt overwhelmed.

Alison became so stressed that she started to develop the physical symptoms of stress. She lost a lot of weight and had trouble sleeping. She became trapped

▶

in the stress loop. Her relationship with her peers and bosses deteriorated, so they left her alone with her stress and started relying on her less.

Unsurprisingly, she finally reached a crisis point at which she had to make a decision. So she took time out for herself one weekend, reacquainted herself with her core values, and remembered her innate abilities. She knew that inside she was a powerful, capable woman, and that how she was reacting wasn't like her – conversely, she was used to being known as a powerhouse.

Something snapped in her to make her realise that she had become a victim in her own job. So she reclaimed her own power. Once she did that, she started operating within the big picture and saw the priorities of the company and her own priorities in terms of the amount of time she was willing to give to the company, and what she needed for her own wellbeing.

She physically became a different person and started making better decisions, and took on the projects that made a difference to the company. She started providing better leadership and became a person to be reckoned with at work.

MENTAL TRAPS

We all have blocks from time to time. Our friends or an observer can easily tell us what we need to do. But when stuck in a mental trap being told doesn't necessarily make a difference, sometimes we need to realise it for ourselves or be coached to see it for ourselves. In the example above, Alison was stuck in a mental trap; her colleagues and boss told her to prioritise her work and communicate what she was and was not able to do. Alison couldn't really see it and was stuck in the trap of having to do it all. She was attempting to get everything done even when it was not possible, or desirable, to do it all. Here are common mental traps that people get into:

False economy of time

We all get trapped here from time to time, when we think we don't have enough time in the day to get everything done. Rather than take a realistic view of what we will get done and what we won't, we forgo all the things that will help us be more productive. We don't take our breaks, we eat lunch at our desk, we skip going to the gym and we work late without taking a break. We throw out all the things we know we should be doing, thinking falsely that by just putting more hours in we'll get everything done. What happens is we become a lot less productive and overworked. This is what I call the false economy of time. It is like a hamster wheel and even when you get off, it is easy to get back into it again. Just remember, when you start thinking like this it is the reptilian brain thinking not the higher brain. Taking the time to plan correctly and keep to a schedule will help you relate to the reality of how long things take to get done.

Fear

Our emotions are another derailment or obstacle. Human beings are naturally wired for fear. Our reptilian brain which operates unconsciously is on a constant lookout for threats. This is why we have survived as a species; our survival mechanism becomes activated in less than a second. The impact is that our brains are always alert for incidents that endanger our survival – not just physically but also the survival of our ego and status. Fear helps us survive. The only problem is we don't do our best work when in fear.

Examples of how we can be ruled by fear are when we work late because we fear that we will be seen as not pulling our weight. In meetings we are afraid to voice our opinions because of fear of what someone might think. We are afraid to leave work on time because we are frightened of our bosses.

Our environment and culture fuel our fears, most of the material on the news or in newspapers is fear-based. There will often be people who will project their fear onto you, such as parents, colleagues, bosses or friends. Whether the fear is justified or not, it is important to notice how the world is wired for fear, and keep some objectivity on it.

Dealing with fear

The first step is to recognise that fear affects a lot of our decisions. When feeling fear the first thing to do is stop and look at what the fear is about and see if it is rational or irrational. Just ask yourself, what is it I'm afraid of?

Anger

There are a few forms of anger. Overt anger doesn't go down well in an Anglo-Saxon work environment but there are other forms of more subtle anger, such as passive aggressiveness, impatience and frustration. Anger takes many forms. There is nothing wrong with getting angry now and again, but if we have too much anger we set off the same physical responses as when getting stressed. You'll notice your heart rate goes up for a start. We are engaging the fight-or-flight response. Hidden anger is usually a fear of loss or missing out on something. Whenever you feel angry, examine what is underneath the anger. What is the underlying fear?

World view

The beliefs we have about ourselves are our context for ourselves and our lives. The world view deeply affects how we act. Often these beliefs are subconscious. For example, in Alison's story we identified the negative belief of not being able to say no. She believed she had to do everything that was asked of her.

CASE STUDY

I used to see the world as a struggle. I used to think that to succeed in life meant I had to struggle. The result was I just made it in life. I left revising at school to the last minute and I only revised to the point where the exam would be a challenge rather than knowing it so well I could teach it. My work habits were to do well until I got some praise; once I was acknowledged I would then slack a bit so that I had the challenge of getting back on track. Subconsciously I was more interested in the challenge and highs and lows of success than

▶

continual improvement. This ultimately kept me stuck in one place; unless I was in an increasingly challenging environment I would stagnate. It used a lot of my energy. It was in recognising this that I was able to give up this way of operating: giving up having to struggle. Life has been a lot less dramatic since.

We don't always have the luxury of time to figure out our negative beliefs, but doing so can make a life-changing difference. I recommend doing this work with a coach whenever you feel that you are stuck in a rut and are not sure how to get out of it.

By looking at the questions on context in the earlier chapters, you can begin to uncover any negative beliefs about yourself.

THE IMPORTANCE OF VALUE

The biggest antidote to fear, anger and negative beliefs is recognising value; this includes your innate value, the value you bring and the value of others. By coming from value you bring a sense of appreciation and positive emotion which can override the negative emotions we can find ourselves in.

Valuing self

The most important thing that every human being needs to learn is to value themselves. You are the centre of your world. If you dropped dead, the world would cease to exist for you! Everyone that you are working for would no longer get the value that you are providing. You are necessary to fulfil your responsibilities. Yes, you are probably replaceable in your job but that doesn't take away from your inherent value. Valuing yourself is the best way to safeguard yourself from stress and keep to set boundaries. It creates a strong foundational rock for your emotional security. When you value yourself, you tend to be less driven by fear and you can start to look at life more objectively and more powerfully. You are less likely to feel pressured into things that don't work for you, for example working late.

Valuing others

It is equally important to value others, especially those closest to you such as your family, friends, co-workers, your organisation. Valuing others means you'll treat them better and won't become egotistical or self-obsessed. You'll start to have more empathy for others and be less likely to get into arguments with others.

Valuing your contribution

Sometimes we forget what difference we are making in our jobs and to the people around us. By having a clear perspective on the value that you bring you can avoid the emotional turmoil that we put ourselves through when we forget who we are. In fact, coming from a value mindset will enable you to look more objectively at what you do. When you value yourself, others and your contribution, you will start to see that you add more value when you are refreshed, alert and firing on all cylinders. You will communicate and think from adding value and move from an hours-based view to an output view. Too many companies are still based on an hours-worked paradigm rather than a value paradigm. So, to summarise: value yourself, others, and your contribution and use.

Getting on with it

OK, now that I've spoken about what is possible and what might get in the way there's no excuse for not taking it on. I recommend getting a buddy to work through the material with you.

Personally, I've experienced many unexpected results from learning how to manage my time and energy. From using the body sensitivity energy techniques I've managed to improve my eyesight: going from having a lot of eye strain and not being able to read without glasses for five minutes to being able to read for about four hours with reading glasses. I'm able to release tension in my neck and shoulders. Many people have used these techniques to get better sleep. One client who suffered from anxiety reported being able to temporarily relieve her heart palpitations by doing the energy exercises. I'm not going to promise that these kinds of results are achievable by everyone but if you keep practising who knows what the results could be.

Resources

There are a number of resources on my website which will enable you to more easily implement some of the techniques in this book. Go to my website **www.energyequationbook.com** for guided meditations for energising, sleep and de-stressing.

CHAPTER 12

Final words

This text has provided you with a lot of background information, explanations, tips and techniques. Like many people who read about personal development (myself included), you might think, 'Oh, that's nice; I'll get a few tips and then move on.'

I intended the information in this text to be put to use to improve your quality of life. My mission is to help you have it all: a great career, success, great relationships, great friendships, health fitness and wealth; whatever you want in life.

By practising the techniques in this text you will improve your physical, emotional and mental wellbeing and have more time for the good things in life.

Personally, I've experienced many unexpected results from the practices here, and I'm nowhere near to being perfect. I'm not the most disciplined person in the world so if I can, anyone can.

So my advice is, keep practising. There is an ancient Chinese proverb: to know and not to do is not to know.

Good Luck!

Index